GEORGIA MADE

THE MOST IMPORTANT FIGURES WHO SHAPED
THE STATE IN THE TWENTIETH CENTURY

NEELY YOUNG

FOREWORD BY SENATOR SAXBY CHAMBLISS

THE
History
PRESS

Published by The History Press
Charleston, SC
www.historypress.com

Copyright © 2021 by Neely Young
All rights reserved

First published 2021

ISBN 9781467150996

Library of Congress Control Number: 2021943802

To my loving wife, Kathy, for her understanding and inspiration.

CONTENTS

CONTENTS

CONTENTS

FOREWORD

Although we did not meet during our college days at the University of Georgia in the mid-1960s, Neely Young and his wonderful wife, Kathy, have been great and dear friends of my wife, Julianne, and me since my early years as a U.S. representative from Georgia's Eighth Congressional District. Our personal and professional paths have often crossed, and our conversations about Georgia history and Georgia's leaders are always part of our shared memories and highlighted those visits. To this day, we have continued our friendship and look forward again to seeing Neely and Kathy this fall to watch the Bulldogs and our South Georgia border rivals, the Florida Gators, in the annual football grudge match better known as the "World's Largest Outdoor Cocktail Party."

From Neely's youth in Cedartown through college in Athens, to Valdosta, Dalton and Marietta as a reporter and publisher of community newspapers and *Georgia Trend* magazine, his integrity, judgment and sincerity were reflected in his extraordinary skills as a writer and a lifelong student of Georgia history and Georgia's leaders and leadership.

Georgia Made is an important literary contribution that tells the story of Georgia's leaders in the twentieth century with inspiration and insight. Significantly, Neely describes their soaring achievements and, when appropriate, their disappointments within the context of their lives, contributions and the times in which they led and lived. I commend Neely for this candid assessment of our leaders. Time does march on. Current debates and arguments about past and present leaders and their accomplishments for good or ill being measured against today's customs and beliefs can be problematical. Such discussions are necessary; however, not to include the circumstances of their historical relevance is too simple and easy and a disservice to the subject and you, the reader.

Neely's timeless study of Georgia's twentieth-century leaders is significant because he writes of events as they happened. His courage as a reporter, editor, publisher and author reflects his lifelong commitment to publishing the truth as he sees it and invites the reader to use their own critical thinking and analyses while reading his anthologies.

I was honored and fortunate to represent the people of Georgia in Congress and the Senate for twenty years. As Neely has done since his early days and throughout his career, I, too, have looked for friends and later colleagues who thought hard about the story, legacy and promise of America. On Capitol Hill, I am still proud that I worked with my partisan colleagues and those across the aisle to agree on the facts and develop legislation that we thought both served our constituents and met the challenges facing Georgia and the nation. We did our best.

In Neely's superb collection of Georgia leaders, he tells their stories with the special insight only he can bring to such a narrative. With his firm grasp of their virtues and foibles, you will gain an understanding of these individuals and Georgia's past through Neely's extraordinary lens. The narrative lights the path again and again for us to help Georgia and the nation heal the very real divisions and meet the challenges that we face today and tomorrow.

Whether the reader is an elected official, CEO, business owner, employee, teacher or student, *Georgia Made* should be on their and every Georgian's bookshelf as a great read.

Many readers will be reminded of Shakespeare's *The Tempest* and the famous playwright's commentary that "the past is prologue." Neely sets the stage for us to lead and shape the future for Georgia and the nation.

Thanks, my friend!

—Senator Saxby Chambliss

ACKNOWLEDGEMENTS

T hank you to those who gave me help and encouragement with preparing my book documenting the most influential Georgians of the twentieth century. I am indebted to Patty Rasmussen for her skillful editing, which gave pace and movement to my prose; Christy Simo for diligent fact-checking; and Heidi Rizzi for chasing down more than one hundred pieces of art and pictures to illustrate the individual stories in the book. I am grateful to those who supplied the material for the book, including the University of Georgia Press, the Mercer University Press, the Georgia Historical Society and the Atlanta History Center. Lastly, I am in debt to special friends who gave me advice in writing the book, including Joe Gartrell, Peggy Galis, Frederick Allen, Micky Blackwell, Senator Saxby Chambliss, Benjamin Neely Young Jr. and many others.

INTRODUCTION

The history of Georgia in the twentieth century is the history of great men and women. Based on my career and experiences living, working and studying Georgia history, I have compiled a list of the people I consider the most influential Georgians of the twentieth century. I became interested in this project as a result of my tenure as editor-in-chief and publisher of *Georgia Trend* magazine, a publication covering business, politics and economic development. *Georgia Trend* enjoys a large statewide circulation and includes stories from different cities and counties. Each year, the January issue selects the most influential citizens from the previous year. For over twenty years, *Georgia Trend* magazine has published this annual issue, and it has continued since my retirement in 2018.

This book names the most influential Georgians of the twentieth century. This effort asks the question: who has had the most significant impact—both good and bad—on our state's history? Many are exceptional people. Some are modest, obscure, famous, flamboyant or reprehensible. But they cannot fail to be interesting.

For instance, in 1971, Jimmy Carter, a peanut farmer from South Georgia, became governor of Georgia. When his term ended, he ran for president of the United States and won.

In 1930, golfer Bobby Jones won the Grand Slam, winning four major golf championships in one year. No one has ever matched this mark, not even Arnold Palmer or Tiger Woods. In 1934, he founded the Augusta National Masters Golf Tournament, which is still the number-one golf event in the world.

In 1913, Georgia governor John Slaton condemned the hanging of Leo Frank, a Jewish man who was sentenced to hang for the murder of thirteen-year-old Mary Phagan, an event that attracted national attention. The governor found no reason for Frank to be hanged for his supposed crime and changed Frank's conviction to life. Although a group of citizens kidnapped Frank and lynched him, Governor Slaton stood tall.

However, some are influential for bad things they did or the evil they incited. In the 1950s and 1960s, Governor Lester Maddox continued Georgia's racist programs that eventually propelled Dr. Martin Luther King, Governor Ernest Vandiver and many others to turn the tide through persistent peaceful protests and legislative action to successfully integrate Georgia schools.

The list includes others in other disciplines, such as University of Georgia coach Vince Dooley, who won the football National Championship in 1980, and business leader Ted Turner, who founded CNN (Cable News Network), which revolutionized the way people consumed news. Johnny Mercer charmed the nation with songs like "Moon River," and Alice Walker won the Pulitzer Prize for writing *The Color Purple*.

This book is not meant to be read as a work of scholarship. It is an evocation of the excitement, pleasures and miseries of the twentieth century, and I hope it is accurate enough to satisfy scholars. It asks that readers be careful when interpreting the actions of people from another century. We should judge them by standards of their time, both good and bad.

You, dear reader, may apply this exercise to form your own list of influential citizens, and your list might be completely different from mine. You may disagree with some of those honored and point out other names that should be listed. If you decide to do this exercise, either by yourself or with friends, it will open for you an important perspective on Georgia events.

Many of those included herein are already in their graves, soon to be joined by all of us, and they will be remembered collectively in the powerful march of Georgia history.

HENRY "HANK" AARON

THE HOME RUN KING OF ALL TIME
FEBRUARY 5, 1934–JANUARY 22, 2021

H ammerin" Hank Aaron broke the baseball home run record set by Yankees great Babe Ruth. By the time his career ended, he had amassed 755 career home runs, playing for the Milwaukee Braves and then moving to Atlanta when the franchise moved in 1966. He finished his career playing for the Milwaukee Brewers.

But the most memorable moment of his career was April 8, 1974, when he hit home run number 715 into the visitors' bullpen in front of a screaming crowd at Atlanta–Fulton County Stadium. He broke Babe Ruth's long-standing home run record and remained the home run leader until the record was broken again in 2007.

Aaron was born during the Depression in Mobile, Alabama, to a poor family of eight children. He was a gifted athlete and played football and baseball in his segregated high school, helping them to win the Mobile Negro High School Baseball State Championship in 1946. Major League Baseball was desegregated in 1947, when Jackie Robinson joined the Brooklyn Dodgers. In 1951, an eighteen-year-old Aaron quit high school to sign a contract with the Indianapolis Clowns, a Negro League team. His .366 batting average helped the Clowns win the 1952 Negro League World Series.

Following the championship in 1952, Aaron received two offers to join the New York Giants and the Boston Braves. He chose the Braves and joined their farm team, ending the season as the Northern League's Rookie of the Year. He went on to win other honors during his farm team years.

Hank Aaron. *MediaPunch/ Shutterstock.*

In 1954, Aaron made his major-league debut with the Braves, who had moved from Boston to Milwaukee the year before. During his first few years, his worth as a player paid big dividends for the team. He won two National League batting titles, led the league in doubles and was named the Sporting News Player of the Year. In 1957, his homer in the eleventh inning clinched a spot for the Braves in the World Series. He then batted .393 and hit three home runs against the New York Yankees, giving the Milwaukee Braves their first World Series title.

In 1966, the year the Braves moved to Atlanta, Aaron hit his 400th career home run and, two years later, hit his 500th home run to move into third place on the all-time career home run list. In 1970, he became the first player to reach both 3,000 hits and 500 home runs. The following year, he hit 40 home runs and increased his total homers to 600. By this time, the national media had begun to cover Aaron's climb toward Babe Ruth's record 714 home runs. He ended the 1973 season with 713, only 1 shy of tying Ruth's record.

The next year, the media frenzy reached a fever pitch. Aaron received more than 900,000 pieces of fan mail, but among the praise and encouragement came letters filled with ugly racial slurs, offensive language and even death threats. The Braves hired bodyguards to sit in the stands, watching Aaron in the outfield in case of trouble. Through it all, Aaron maintained a quiet, reserved approach to the attention.

During the 1974 season, against the Dodgers and in front of 53,775 fans, Aaron broke Ruth's record. Dodgers radio announcer Vin Scully told his national listeners, "A Black man is getting a standing ovation in the Deep South for breaking a record of an all-time baseball idol. What a marvelous moment for baseball. What a marvelous moment for Atlanta and the state of Georgia, What a marvelous moment for the country and the world!"

The Braves announcer Milo Hamilton called the game on WSB radio and described the scene: "Henry Aaron, in the second inning walked and scored. He's sitting on 714. Here's the pitch by Downing. Swinging. There's a drive into left-center field. That ball is gonna be-eee…Outta here! It's gone! It's 715! There's a new home run champion of all time, and it's Henry

Aaron! The fireworks are going. Henry Aaron is coming around third. His teammates are at home plate. And listen to the crowd!"

Aaron scored 2,174 runs in his career and remains the all-time leader in runs batted in (RBI) with 2,297 and 6,856 total bases. His 12,364 at-bats are currently the second-highest total ever. After retiring, he became an executive vice president of the Atlanta Braves, including working with player development and encouraging minority hiring in baseball.

In 1982, Aaron was inducted into the National Baseball Hall of Fame. In 2000, he was named to Major League Baseball's All-Century Team. President Bill Clinton awarded him the Presidential Citizen Medal, and in 2002, he was given the Presidential Medal of Freedom by President George Bush.

He retired in Atlanta with his wife, Billye, and his six children. Aaron was a successful businessman and owned several car dealerships and other businesses. He was a civil rights leader and an inspiration to young people all over the South. Boxing legend Muhammad Ali called Aaron "the only man I idolize more than myself."

After he broke the home run record, fans commissioned a bronze monument of Aaron swinging a bat. The number 715 was engraved on the base. The statue stands near the site of Atlanta–Fulton County stadium. And though his record was broken in 2007, in Atlanta and the hearts and minds of his fans, Aaron's record still stands.

Sources

Aaron, Hank, with Lonnie Wheeler. *I Had a Hammer: The Hank Aaron Story*. New York: HarperCollins, 1991.

Johnson, Bill. "Hank Aaron." The Society of American Baseball Research. www. sabr.org.

ROBERT SENGSTACKE ABBOTT

THE FATHER OF BLACK JOURNALISM
NOVEMBER 24, 1870–FEBRUARY 29, 1940

Robert Abbott was an African American born on St. Simons Island to former slaves Thomas and Flora Abbott. His father died when he was a baby, and his widowed mother married a man named John Sengstacke. Sengstacke raised Abbott as if he were his own child, giving him his middle name—Sengstacke. His stepfather was a Congregational missionary and the publisher of the *Woodville Times*, a local newspaper near Savannah.

Robert studied printing at the Hampton Institute, a Black college in Virginia, and then earned a law degree from Kent College of Law in Chicago. When he returned to Georgia, he discovered that thousands of African Americans were leaving the South and moving north, where more jobs were available. At the time, Blacks were segregated in Georgia and other states in the Deep South and suffered under Jim Crow laws that denied them equal voting rights and other constitutional rights available to those in the North.

Abbott moved back to Chicago and founded the *Chicago Defender*, a Black newspaper advocating for social justice that encouraged readers to leave the South. The *Defender* became the largest Black-owned newspaper in America. It started with a circulation of 50,000 and grew to more than 200,000 by the 1920s.

Through the *Defender*'s work, Abbott contributed to the "Great Migration," the movement of more than 1.5 million rural southern blacks to cities in the North and Midwest. The *Defender* published stories that showed pictures of

Newspaper founder Robert S. Abbott (*right*) checking copy fresh from the printing press at the African American newspaper the *Chicago Defender. Gordon Coster/The LIFE Picture Collection/Shutterstock.*

Chicago as a place of prosperity and justice, and the publication included classified ads for housing and job openings.

The slogan of the newspaper was "American racial prejudice must be destroyed." Abbott listed nine goals as the *Defender* "Bible," including government schools giving preference to American citizens before foreigners, federal legislation to abolish lynching, gaining representation in all departments of the police force throughout the United States and full enfranchisement for all American citizens.

Abbott's success made him a millionaire and one of the richest Black men in America. He used his wealth to help people, sending money back to his native state. During the 1930s, he assisted many Black children in Georgia, paying for their education. Abbott died in Chicago and is buried in Oak Woods Cemetery there. A historical marker indicates where his childhood home once stood in Savannah, and the Chicago Defender Building became a city landmark in 1998.

Source

Engle, Susan. *Change Maker Robert Sengstacke Abbott: A Man, a Paper, and a Parade.* Wilmette, IL: Bellwood Press, 2019.

MAYOR IVAN ALLEN JR.

PRAISED FOR HIS COURAGE
MARCH 15, 1911–JULY 2, 2003

Ivan E. Allen Jr. was the fifty-second mayor of Atlanta and led the city during the civil rights struggle in the 1960s. He was responsible for changing the Old South city into a progressive, prosperous New South city.

He was born in Atlanta, attended Boys High School and graduated from Georgia Tech University cum laude in 1933. After college, he went to work for his father's office supply business. He worked with the company for many years and became president in 1946. Allen grew the company and soon had more than two hundred employees and became the region's top office supply and furniture dealer, with seventeen offices throughout the South.

He was active in community affairs, including serving as president of the local and state chambers of commerce. He ran for governor twice as a segregationist candidate but lost both those races. Convinced that the South could not thrive economically under segregation, he changed his philosophy, supporting equal rights for Black people.

In 1961, Allen ran for mayor of Atlanta against arch-segregationist Lester Maddox and won by a large margin. His progressive, positive campaign message garnered support from white citizens and the Black community. When he moved into city hall, he ordered all "Colored" and "White" signs removed and desegregated the cafeteria.

For the next eight years under his leadership, the city's population grew by over 30 percent. During his term, he made significant changes that affected the trajectory of the city and still reverberate today. His support of the Atlanta International Airport grew the airport from tenth in the nation to the country's third busiest (at that time). He oversaw construction of the Atlanta–Fulton County Stadium and convinced the Milwaukee Braves to move to Atlanta in 1965. The Atlanta Falcons and Atlanta Hawks were also established during his tenure. And he oversaw the early phases of construction on I-285 and the Downtown Connector during his term.

He was praised for his boldness by both Black and white citizens. In 1966, a white policeman shot a Black resident in south Atlanta, and a riot broke out. Mayor Allen drove to the scene and tried to calm the crowd. He stood on the hood of a police car urging Black protesters to go home. When the crowd rocked the vehicle, he was thrown off the car, got on his feet and

Ivan Allen. *AP/Shutterstock.*

continued trying to appease the group. Major newspapers and televisions covered the event.

When civil rights leader Dr. Martin Luther King Jr. won the Nobel Peace Prize in 1964, Allen organized a banquet to honor him that was attended by 1,500 people, both white and Black. In the days following King's assassination in Memphis in 1968, riots broke out across the country. Allen joined other leaders to ensure the city of Atlanta remained peaceful when nearly 200,000 people came to the funeral.

While other cities and states in the South used their state patrols to keep Black students from entering public colleges and universities, Atlanta worked to find a peaceful path to integration. In 1963, President John F. Kennedy asked Allen to testify before Congress about how Atlanta maintained positive race relations.

In his speech to both the House of Representatives and Senate, Allen conveyed his support of a federal law mandating making public accommodations available to Black people. Major newspapers pointed out that he was the only southern mayor to speak out on behalf of what became the Civil Rights Act of 1964.

When Allen left office, he was credited with making Atlanta a "City Too Busy to Hate," a term coined during Mayor William Hartsfield's tenure. Georgia Tech renamed the liberal arts college in his name and established the Ivan Allen Jr. Prize for Social Courage in his honor. He received honorary degrees from many colleges, including Morris Brown College, Emory University, Morehouse College and Davidson College. Allen went on to advocate for social change until his death at age ninety-two.

Sources

Allen, Ivan, Jr., and Paul Hemphill. *Mayor: Notes on the Sixties*. New York: Simon and Schuster, 1971.

Galloway, Tammy H. "Ivan Allen, Jr." New Georgia Encyclopedia, August 23, 2004. www.georgiaencyclopedia.org.

Martin, Douglas. Obituary for Ivan Allen Jr. *New York Times*, July 2, 2003. www.nytimes.com/2003/07/02/obituaries/ivan-allen-exmayor-of-atlanta-dies-at-92.html.

WILLIAM G. ANDERSON

See entry for Mayor Malcolm Maclean (page 116).

GOVERNOR ROY BARNES

CHANGED THE GEORGIA STATE FLAG, COMMITTING POLITICAL SUICIDE
MARCH 11, 1948–

Democrat Roy E. Barnes was called the "most powerful Georgia governor in history" by many, but he lost his reelection bid to a Republication because he had the courage to change the state flag from the Confederate Stars and Bars to one that was more appropriate for a modern state.

Barnes was born in Mableton and grew up working on his father's farm and at the community hardware store. He attended the University of Georgia and graduated with his law degree in 1972.

After graduation, he served in the Cobb County district attorney's office. He ran for political office in 1974 and was elected to the Georgia Senate as one of the youngest candidates to serve the state. He was popular and had a down-home style that resonated with voters. He served for eight terms, during which he was named chairman of the Senate Judiciary Committee and served as floor leader for Governor Joe Frank Harris. Barnes ran for governor in 1990, losing to Zell Miller. He returned to the legislature, winning a seat in the state House of Representatives, where he became the House Judiciary Committee vice chairman.

In 1998, he ran for governor and won. His first act was to try to improve the state's education system. Barnes was popular with his fellow members in the House and Senate and knew how to use his skill and knowledge of the legislative process to move his agenda forward. But it was his efforts to change the Georgia flag for which he's best remembered.

In the 1950s, segregation was the law of the land. But in 1954, the U.S. Supreme Court ruled that separate but equal schools were unconstitutional through the landmark decision of *Brown v. Board of Education*. States were ordered to integrate Black and white schools. Most Georgia political leaders bitterly denounced the new law, and then-governor Marvin Griffin planned to resist the federally imposed integration of Georgia schools.

In protest, the state legislature changed the state flag during the 1956 legislative session to include the Confederate Stars and Bars across two-thirds of the flag to show the world that Georgia leaders would fight to

Roy Barnes. *John Bazemore/AP/ Shutterstock.*

keep legal segregation in schools. Though Georgia schools were peacefully integrated, Governor Griffin's flag continued to fly throughout the state for almost fifty years.

Governor Barnes agreed with most voters that the flag needed to be changed, and in 2001, he proposed a new flag. The new design featured Georgia's gold seal on a blue background with images of six small flags flown over Georgia during its history. It looked like a good compromise because one of the flags was Griffin's Confederate 1956 flag. To placate rural, traditional legislators, a provision in the law protected Confederate monuments on public property, including the giant Stone Mountain carving of Jefferson Davis and Generals Robert E. Lee and Stonewall Jackson.

After the law passed, many conservative voters were outraged by the change, especially because there was no voter input on the new flag. Assorted groups rallied to oppose the new flag, including the Sons of Confederate Veterans, the Georgia Heritage Preservation Association and those who disagreed with Barnes. Called "flaggers," they promoted a "Boot Barnes" movement, with "Boot Barnes" yard signs, bumper stickers and flagpoles flying the Confederate flag at homes in mostly rural parts of the state.

As Barnes ramped up his reelection campaign, flaggers showed up at his events. During his introduction, flaggers would stand up, wave the Georgia Confederate flag and turn their backs on Barnes. His Republican challenger, Sonny Perdue, made the flag a campaign issue and pledged to give people a chance to vote for a new flag. On Election Day, Barnes lost the election to Perdue. (A referendum was indeed held on a new flag design that did not include the Confederate flag emblem, and more than 73 percent preferred the new version over the one adopted during Roy Barnes's term. It was approved in 2004 and flies above the state capitol today.)

During his time in office, Barnes gathered the support of the public, business community and other advocates; pushed education reforms; and organized significant government changes to make Georgia a better place to live. After the election, he left the governor's office and rejoined his law practice, the Barnes Group.

Still trying to make a difference, he ran as a Democrat for governor in 2010 and lost to Republican Nathan Deal. Barnes received many honors and awards for his public service accomplishments, including the national Profile in Courage Award from the John F. Kennedy Library. Though it ended his political career, he was honored for his success in taking the Confederate battle emblem off the Georgia state flag.

Sources

Fennessy, Steve. "Roy Barnes on the Confederate Flag and Where the South Needs to Go from Here." *Atlanta Magazine*, September 25, 2015. atlantamagazine.com.

Jackson, Edwin L. "State Flags of Georgia." New Georgia Encyclopedia, July 26, 2004. www.georgiaencyclopedia.org.

National Governor's Association. "Roy Barnes." www.nga.org.

WRIGHT BAZEMORE

THE GREATEST HIGH SCHOOL FOOTBALL COACH
AUGUST 1, 1916–JUNE 22, 1999

Wright Bazemore was the greatest high school football coach in Georgia. Over twenty-eight seasons as the Valdosta Wildcats coach, he compiled 268 wins, with 51 losses and 7 ties (an 83.28 winning percentage). His teams won 14 state championships and 3 national championships.

His football legacy began in 1934, when, as a teenage quarterback for the high school in Fitzgerald, Georgia, he scored ten touchdowns in two back-to-back games. The popular newspaper feature "Ripley's Believe It or Not" recognized this feat. He went on to play for the Mercer University football team.

In 1946, he took over the high school football program in Valdosta, then a small town just north of the Georgia-Florida state line. Defense was the basis of Bazemore's coaching, and many a team found itself stonewalled when it tried to move the ball. He was an offensive coaching genius and paved the way for many innovations used in college and pro formations today.

He was the first to use the belly play system, where the quarterback takes the ball and hands it to the fullback or, if the quarterback finds the fullback stopped, throws it to the halfback, who runs the ball around the end for a touchdown. This system is commonly used by teams today. He invented the tackle-eligible play, where the quarterback passes to the tackle, much to the defense's surprise. He also developed the center-eligible play that was so successful that it was banned from future games.

AUGUST WRIGHT BAZEMORE

AUGUST WRIGHT BAZEMORE WAS INDUCTED INTO THE
GEORGIA ATHLETIC COACHES ASSOCIATION HALL OF FAME
ON JUNE 9, 2001. HE WAS THE HEAD FOOTBALL COACH AT
VALDOSTA HIGH SCHOOL FOR THIRTY YEARS. HIS RECORD
DURING THAT PERIOD WAS 268 WINS-51 LOSSES, WINNING 3
NATIONAL CHAMPIONSHIPS, 14 STATE CHAMPIONSHIPS,
14 SECTIONAL CHAMPIONSHIPS, 17 REGION CHAMPIONSHIPS,
AND WAS STATE RUNNER-UP 4 TIMES. COACH BAZEMORE AND
THE VALDOSTA WILDCAT FOOTBALL TEAMS HAVE SET THE
STANDARD FOR SUCCESS IN HIGH SCHOOL FOOTBALL IN THE
STATE OF GEORGIA.

Augustus Wright Bazemore, plaque from the Georgia Coach's Hall of Fame, Dalton, Georgia. *Bucky McCamy*.

During the civil rights era, Bazemore actively promoted Black players on his teams. Bazemore put in the first Black player who ever played for the Wildcats near the end of a state championship game against a team in Marietta, Georgia. The player caught the ball in the end zone and ran a one-hundred-yard kickoff return for a touchdown, winning the game and the state championship.

Bazemore was called a southern gentleman who did not curse, drink or smoke. He used his coaching style to train his players to be men of character. Bazemore retired in 1971 and stayed at the school as athletic director before fully retiring in 1980. He was the winningest football coach in Georgia history at the time, winning more than 200 games. He also coached other high school sports, compiling a 176-22 record in basketball, including the state championship in 1947 and six state championship tennis teams.

Bazemore was inducted into several sports halls of fame, including the Georgia Sports Hall of Fame, the Mercer Hall of Fame, the National

Sports Hall of Fame and the Georgia Athletic Coaches Hall of Fame. In 2014, MaxPreps called Wright Bazemore the top football coach in the nation in the 1960s.

After his death in 1999, the football field at Valdosta High School was renamed Bazemore-Hyder Stadium for one of the greatest, if not *the* greatest, high school coaches in Georgia's history.

Sources

Burns, Gabe. "The King of Titletown." *Valdosta Daily Times*, July 11, 2016.

Georgia Hall of Fame. "Wright Bazemore, Inducted in 1960." gshf.org.

Jubera, Drew. *Must Win: A Season of Survival for a Town and Its Team*. New York: St. Martin's Press, 2012.

GRIFFIN BELL

CITIZEN, SOLDIER, LAWYER, JUDGE, ATTORNEY
GENERAL OF THE UNITED STATES
OCTOBER 31, 1918–JANUARY 5, 2009

G riffin Bell served as attorney general of the United States under President Jimmy Carter. He was born in Americus and attended Mercer University, where he graduated with a law degree in 1948. Bell practiced law in Savannah and Rome and then moved to Atlanta in 1953 to join the firm of Spalding Sibley Troutman and Kelley (later renamed King & Spalding).

In 1959, he became chief of staff to Governor Ernest Vandiver. He made a name for himself with his successful efforts to help Governor Vandiver during the civil rights period of the 1950s and 1960s. President John F. Kennedy appointed Bell to the U.S. Court of Appeals for the Fifth Circuit in 1961. He served there until 1976, when he was tapped by Carter to serve as attorney general.

When he was on the federal court, Bell took a stand in a dispute in the Georgia gubernatorial election of 1966, when the results showed the vote was a tie between Democrat Lester Maddox and Republican Howard "Bo" Callaway. Maddox believed in segregationist laws preventing Blacks from attending white schools and segregating other facilities. He was a known eccentric who once kicked Black ministers out of his chicken restaurant. Local newspapers ran pictures of him using axe handles to beat African Americans. Callaway was more liberal and had more support from the state business elite.

Current laws at the time put the election in the hands of the legislature, which was controlled by the Democrats, meaning Maddox would surely win

Griffin Bell. *Library of Congress.*

the election. By federal order, Bell struck down the provision requiring that the legislature choose the governor. The famous ruling went all the way to the U.S. Supreme Court, which overruled Bell's order, paving the way for Maddox being named governor.

As attorney general, Bell always addressed policy decisions he thought were grounded in fundamental law, even when he disagreed with President Carter. In one instance, Bell refused to pursue a federal prosecution sought by President Carter in a case involving the police and the death of a twelve-year-old boy. Bell told Carter that the president's only solution was to change attorneys general.

In trying to repair the Watergate scandals of the Nixon era, Bell announced the indictment of Acting FBI Director L. Patrick Gray for authorizing the break-in by New York political activists. Bell introduced requirements that any authorized illegal activities must be in writing. And he was credited with opening the ranks of federal prosecutors and judges to women and minority attorneys.

After leaving the attorney general's office, he returned to his old firm at King & Spalding and practiced law for thirty years. His legal work was notable, including representing a man whose capture by Nicaraguan authorities exposed the Iran-Contra scandal. He took cases opposing segregation and racial quotas and was a strong defender of the First Amendment. In later years, he was named to a commission to review the Defense Department and other agencies mining personal information from private citizens.

Before his death in 2004, he received many honors and was considered the dean of Georgia lawyers. He passed away at age ninety and is buried in his hometown of Americus. His tombstone reads, "Citizen Soldier, Trial Lawyer, Federal Appellate Judge, Attorney General of the United States."

Sources

Lyons, Patrick J. "Griffin Bell, Ex–Attorney General, Dies at 90." *New York Times*, January 5, 2009.

Murphy, Reg. *Uncommon Sense*. Atlanta: Longstreet Press, 1999.

MARTHA BERRY

M artha Berry was the founder of Berry College, a liberal arts college located in Rome, Georgia. At an early age, she wanted to help children of poor tenant farmers who had no way to learn math, writing and other basic education skills. Her father, a wealthy merchant, was also concerned about the plight of poor farmers near their home, Oak Hill, outside Rome. She opened a high school for boys and girls in an abandoned church to help them.

Her school started with only four students and was open to those who were willing to study and work the land around her father's 150-acre farm that surrounded the school. Today, that first school has grown into a four-year college, with more than two thousand students and the nation's most extensive work-study program.

Her philosophy was to teach Appalachian boys and girls educational skills and modern agricultural farming training. She had a fourfold approach that included "Bible for prayer, the lamp for learning, the plow for labor and the cabin for simplicity." She chose as the school motto, "Not to be ministered unto but to minister."

During the Depression in the 1930s, times were hard for the school. Berry sent a letter to auto magnate Henry Ford asking for his support. The story goes that Ford sent her a dime. Discouraged, she took the dime to a feed store and purchased ten cents worth of peanuts. The students planted the peanuts, and at the end of the season, she harvested the crop and sold it for $1,500. Berry deposited the money, then wrote out a $1,500 check, which

Martha Berry bust
in Berry College Log
Cabin yearbook,
1951. *Courtesy of
the Georgia Historical
Society*.

MARTHA BERRY
FOUNDER
October 7, 1866
February 27, 1942

Bust of Miss Martha Berry owned by The Berry Schools.

she sent to Ford along with a note that read: "Mr. Ford, Here is your $1,500 return for your dime invested in Berry College." She noted that the peanuts were grown by her students.

Ford was so surprised that he took a train to Rome and met her. He watched her students work and study, and he was so impressed that he gave her $3 million. With the donation from Ford, Berry was able to increase her efforts for the boys' school and start a school for girls. Ford gave more than $4 million to the school, and his donations encouraged others to help Berry raise more than $25 million. Andrew Carnegie gave her a $50,000 endowment, and other donors added to that total. President Woodrow Wilson and his wife, Ellen Axson Wilson, who was from Rome, helped her expand, but most of the school's financial support came from women's groups and small anonymous donors. Her school grew, and by 1929, it included 129 buildings on twenty-seven thousand acres.

Berry became a national figure in education and was presented the Roosevelt Medal by President Calvin Coolidge. Other honors include honorary doctorates by the University of Georgia, Duke University and the University of North Carolina. The Georgia General Assembly honored her, and she was the first woman appointed to Georgia's Board of Regents.

After she died in 1942, Berry continued to receive honors. A portion of Highway 21 in Rome was named the Martha Berry Highway, and her portrait hangs in the Georgia Capitol Gallery of Distinguished Georgians. Today, the college has nearly two thousand students, and 99 percent of its professors hold a PhD. The campus is called the most beautiful college in America, and *U.S. News and World Report* has named Berry University one of the best universities in the South.

Sources

Berry College. "Martha Berry." www.berry.edu/about/our-rich-history/martha-berry.

Byers, Tracy. *Martha Berry: The Sunday Lady of Possum Trot*. New York: G.P. Putnam's Sons, 1932.

ARTHUR BLANK

See entry for Bernie Marcus (page 124).

FEDERAL JUDGE AUGUSTUS "GUS" BOOTLE

See entry for Mayor Malcolm Maclean (page 116).

JAMES BROWN

THE GODFATHER OF SOUL
MAY 3, 1933–DECEMBER 25, 2006

Dubbed the "Godfather of Soul," James Brown was a significant figure in the twentieth century as a singer, songwriter and band director. He was born in South Carolina and sent to live with his aunt in Augusta when he was four years old. He was involved in petty crime around the Augusta area and spent several years in prison, both as a teenager and an adult.

After his release from prison, he got involved with a band called the Gospel Starlighters. Brown quickly dominated the group with his vocals and presence, and they soon renamed themselves the Famous Flames. They performed local concerts and at events at universities and colleges across the South.

In 1956, the Flames recorded their first song in the basement of a local radio station in Augusta. The song, titled "Please, Please, Please," was picked up by King Records, which signed the Flames to a contract. The band rerecorded the song in a studio in Cincinnati, and then the record company sent the song to stations across the country. It was a major hit, staying on the R&B chart for over a year and selling millions of copies.

The Flames' next recording, "Try Me," went to number one on the rhythm-and-blues chart. The band made a tour across the nation, where the Flames songs featured wild rock-and-roll music. The end of the show featured Brown's routine of collapsing onstage, having a cape thrown over him and tossing it away for one more encore, again and again. Brown appeared at concerts all over the United States, including New York's famed Apollo Theater in Harlem.

James Brown. *Roland Kemp/ Shutterstock.*

In the '70s, '80s and '90s, Brown wrote hit after hit, including "I Got You [I Feel Good]," "Hot Pants," "Give It Up and Turn It Loose" and "Super Bad." In 1980, he appeared in the movie *The Blues Brothers* with the actor John Belushi, and in 1985, he recorded "Living in America" for the film *Rocky 4*, earning him a Grammy Award for Best R&B Recording. In 1986, Brown was inducted into the Rock and Roll Hall of Fame as a member of its inaugural class alongside such greats as Chuck Berry, Ray Charles and Little Richard.

In 1992, Brown received a Lifetime Achievement Award at the Grammy Awards. He was a Kennedy Center Honoree in 2003 and received the BET Lifetime Achievement Award in 2003, presented by Michael Jackson.

He never left his roots (he remained in the Augusta area), but he lived a tumultuous life, including arrests for driving under the influence, discharging a rifle during a car chase and having continuing battles with the IRS over his taxes. Brown donated to many good causes in the Augusta region and was a part of the city's annual Christmas toy giveaway.

He always said, "I'm the hardest working man in show business, and I'm not going to let them down." A bronze statue of Brown placed by the City of Augusta stands at the center of Main Street with a plaque that reads: "James Brown, The Godfather of Soul."

Sources

Biography. "James Brown: The Godfather of Soul." www.biography.com.

Rock and Roll Hall of Fame. "James Brown." www.rockhall.com.

Smith, R.J. *The One: The Life and Music of James Brown*. New York: Penguin Random House, 2012.

GEORGE L. CAGLE

See entry for Jesse Jewell (page 94).

ERSKINE CALDWELL

WROTE STARK NOVELS OF THE SOUTH
DECEMBER 17, 1903–APRIL 11, 1987

E rskine Caldwell was a Georgia author who wrote more than 25 novels, 12 nonfiction books and 150 shorts, mostly about his experiences with poor farmers and factory workers in the South and their struggles with poverty in the time of racial integration. His most well-known books, *Tobacco Road* and *God's Little Acre*, were bestsellers and made into movies in the 1930s. The two books sold more than seventeen million copies and made him famous and wealthy.

Caldwell was born in Moreland. His father, Ira Sylvester Caldwell, was a Presbyterian minister who traveled and preached in small towns across the South before settling in the community of Wrens, near Augusta. The young Caldwell attended Erskine College, the University of Pennsylvania and the University of Virginia but didn't earn a degree. Instead, he left school to take a job as a reporter at the *Atlanta Journal*.

In 1932, Caldwell wrote *Tobacco Road* about a poor family in Georgia struggling to make ends meet. It was a major success and was made into a play and movie. In 1933, he wrote his acclaimed novel *God's Little Acre*, which described an uneducated farming family in Georgia. The family members are obsessed with wealth and sex. The sexual themes in the plot were controversial for its time. Once, Caldwell was even arrested at a book signing. But the novel became an international bestseller and was adapted into a 1958 film.

Erskine Caldwell. *Library of Congress.*

Despite the controversy surrounding the sexual topics raised in *God's Little Acre* and other works, Caldwell's focus on issues like social injustice, class and race in his writing was distinctive. Caldwell was sometimes called a traitor to his native region because of the way he depicted the South and southerners, but he was still beloved by those who praised his talent.

His disappointment with the government's treatment of poor whites led him to write and publish other novels and short stories, many of which were banned from schools and libraries. In later years, he became a foreign correspondent and traveled to Russia and Ukraine, documenting war efforts there.

Caldwell was married four times. He collaborated with his second wife, famed photojournalist Margaret Bourke-White, on a series of three photo books titled *You Have Seen Their Faces*. The first edition was set in the rural South; the other two documented eastern European countries.

Caldwell was a prolific writer. He wrote 25 novels, close to 150 short stories and 2 autobiographies and edited the American Folkways series of 28 books about different regions of the United States. Caldwell died on April 11, 1987, at age eighty-three of lung cancer. He was buried near his family's home in Ashland, Oregon, despite never having lived there himself. The house in Moreland where he was born is now a museum.

Sources

Caldwell, Erskine. *Brown Thrasher Books.* Athens: University of Georgia Press, 1995, foreword edition.

New York Times. "Erskine Caldwell, 83, Is Dead; Wrote Stark Novels of South." April 13, 1987, A, 3.

PRESIDENT JAMES E. "JIMMY" CARTER

THE COUNTRY'S BEST EX-PRESIDENT
OCTOBER 1, 1924-

James Earl Carter put the small town of Plains, Georgia, on the map. The son of a peanut farmer, Carter graduated from the U.S. Naval Academy in 1946 and served as a submarine officer on a nuclear vessel. He resigned his commission due to his father's death in 1953, and he and his wife, Rosalynn, returned to Plains, taking over the family farm. Then, in what has been called one of the shortest political careers in history—just fourteen years—Carter served in the Georgia Senate (1962), as governor (1971) and as president of the United States (1976).

As governor, Carter reorganized the state government budgeting process into a system called "zero-based budgeting." He championed civil rights and appointed more Black people to leadership positions in state agencies than past governors. He was an advocate for the environment and worked to make government more transparent to the public.

To the surprise of many Georgians, Carter announced plans to run for president of the United States in 1974. He enlisted the help of many Georgians to form a "Peanut Brigade" to campaign throughout the country and won the Democratic nomination. He ran against President Gerald Ford and bested Ford during three debates, where he stated, "I will never lie to the American people." Carter won the election in 1976 with 50.1 percent of the vote and 297 electoral votes versus 48 percent and 240 electoral votes for Ford.

Carter faced many problems during his term in office, including high inflation, which caused interest rates to reach over 18 percent. The recession caused gas prices to climb, and there were long lines at gas stations.

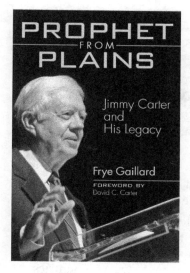

President Jimmy Carter: Prophet from Plains, by Frye Gaillard (University of Georgia Press, 2007).

His limited popularity took hits on several fronts. To help the environment, his administration stopped building dams in parts of the western states, deregulated the trucking and airline industries and expanded the National Park System. Some of these actions caused job losses and other problems that angered those who had elected him.

Carter did better with foreign affairs. He helped broker a historic Middle East peace deal between Egypt and Israel—the Camp David Accords. He signed the Panama Canal treaties, established better relations with China and achieved favorable negotiation of the SALT-II treaty, limiting nuclear weapons with the Soviet Union.

However, during the last fourteen months of his term, Carter faced his most serious setback. In 1979, the nation of Iran seized sixty-six U.S. embassy staffers and held fifty-two of them hostage for more than a year. Negotiations stalled when a rescue mission failed to free the hostages. The American people saw Carter as a weak president unable to solve the crisis.

With the deteriorating economy, high unemployment and inflation and the ongoing media coverage of the hostage crisis during the 1980 presidential campaign, Carter's polling numbers took a significant slide.

His Republican opponent was Ronald Reagan, who campaigned on the notion that "America was losing faith in itself." He promised America that he would bring economic recovery, new jobs and more respect in the world. Reagan won the election in a landslide, receiving the highest number of electoral votes ever won by a non-incumbent presidential candidate, 489 votes to Carter's 49. The Iran hostage crisis ended when the hostages were released on January 20, just minutes after Reagan was inaugurated.

Carter returned to Plains defeated. But despite his record as president, the next chapter in his life became a textbook for how ex-presidents use their influence. Carter became a well-respected humanitarian who changed lives throughout the world.

In 1982, the Carters created the Carter Center, and in 1986, they dedicated the Carter Presidential Library and Museum in Atlanta. The center gave

Carter a platform to focus attention on conflict resolution worldwide and helped Carter become a force for peace, democracy and global health.

The Carter Center has observed more than forty-seven elections in twenty-four countries and assisted the democratic process worldwide. The center has helped broker peace in the Middle East, Korea, Bosnia, Uganda, Sudan, Ethiopia and many other countries. It has strengthened international human rights programs and encouraged standards for those defending democracy in their communities.

Carter pioneered public healthcare delivery systems in African communities and established a coalition that virtually eradicated Guinea worm disease. The center helped control other conditions and advanced mental healthcare, improving the lives of people living with mental illness.

He partnered with Habitat for Humanity, a nonprofit dedicated to building homes for low-income families in need. He and Rosalynn have worked with more than 100,000 volunteers in fourteen countries to renovate more than 4,300 homes.

The Carters have authored numerous books. Jimmy Carter wrote *Palestine: Peace Not Apartheid*, *White House Diary*, *Faith: A Journey for All* and *The Hornet's Nest: A Novel of the Revolutionary War*. Rosalynn has authored *First Lady from Plains*, *Helping Someone with Mental Illness* and *Helping Yourself and Others*.

Carter received numerous awards for his service. In 2002, the Nobel Committee chose Carter to receive the Nobel Peace Prize for his "decades of untiring effort to find peaceful solutions to international conflicts, to advance democracy and human rights, and to promote economic and social development."

When he delivered his speech accepting the award, he concluded: "The bond of our common humanity is stronger than the divisiveness of our fears and prejudices. God gives us the capacity for choice. We can choose to alleviate suffering. We can choose to work together for peace. We can make these changes—and we must."

Sources

DeGregorio, William A. *The Complete Book of U.S. Presidents*. Norwalk, CT: Easton Press, 2002.

Gaillard, Frye. *Prophet from Plains: Jimmy Carter and His Legacy*. Athens: University of Georgia Press, 2007.

S. TRUETT CATHY

CHICK-FIL-A IS STILL CLOSED ON SUNDAY
MARCH 14, 1921–SEPTEMBER 8, 2014

Truett Cathy is most famous for founding the Chick-fil-A restaurant chain, one of the premier fast-food franchises in the United States in annual sales.

His first eating establishment opened in 1946 in the city of Hapeville, just south of Atlanta. He named the restaurant the Dwarf Grill—later renamed the Dwarf House—because the building was so small. It was there in his restaurant in 1964 that Cathy invented his unique chicken sandwich. The recipe called for a fried chicken breast with two pickles on a toasted, buttered bun. The dish was so popular that Cathy started other restaurants serving the dish and named his venture Chick-fil-A.

Cathy had great vision. He located his Chick-fil-A restaurants inside the center of shopping malls, even before food courts were included. Eventually, Chick-fil-A restaurants were in malls all over the South, and in 1986, the company opened its first stand-alone restaurant in Atlanta.

Cathy also decided to close his restaurants on Sundays. When he opened his first restaurant on a Tuesday, Cathy found that he was tired and worn out by Sunday. He worried that many of his customers in the South were not interested in eating out on Sunday and would prefer to attend church and spend the day with their families. A deeply religious man, Cathy never regretted his decision to close on Sunday. He used this time teaching Sunday school for over fifty years.

To lure customers away from fast-food burger chains, Chick-fil-A produced TV, billboard and newspaper ads using Holsteins cows holding signs that said

S. Truett Cathy. *Jennifer Stalcup Photography.*

"EAT MOR CHIKIN." The theme promoted the idea that the renegade cows had trouble with spelling but were smart enough to understand self-preservation. Launched in 1995, the campaign became a hit. The company entered a partnership with the Peach Bowl, the annual football game, in 1996, and the Chick-fil-A cows reached a national audience of over four million people.

Sales for Chick-fil-A chicken sandwiches soared, and the company is now the largest privately owned fast-service restaurant in the country. As of 2021, there were more than 2,669 Chick-fil-A establishments in forty-seven states, with sales of over $13.7 billion in 2020.

In 1984, Cathy founded the WinShape Foundation to provide programs that would impact young people and families and enhance their Christian faith, character and relationships. The foundation's mission states, "We are the Christian non-profit known for creating space for transformation through every phase of life."

The first WinShape initiative built a foster care home at Berry College in Rome, Georgia. The home provided housing for twelve students and two foster parents and created youth-supported programs and scholarships to the college. Named WinShape Homes, the program now has eight foster homes established in Georgia, Alabama and Tennessee. The foundation also created WinShape Camps, with more than forty thousand campers each summer. Cathy's vision was for them to learn leadership skills to be successful in life. Scholarships valued at up to $32,000, jointly funded by WinShape and Berry College, are awarded to up to thirty students annually.

Cathy received many awards over the years, including the William E. Simon Prize for Philanthropic Leadership, the Norman Vincent and Ruth Stafford Peale Humanitarian Award, the Cecil B. Day Ethics Award and the Horatio Alger Award. He wrote several best-selling books, including *It's Easier to Succeed Than to Fail*, *Eat Mor Chikin: Inspire More People* and *It's Better to Build Boys Than Mend Men*.

Cathy retired in 2013 and died at his home at age ninety-three in 2014. Chick-fil-A restaurants are among his legacy, and they are still closed on Sundays.

Sources

Cathy, Truett. *Eat Mor Chikin: Inspire More People*. N.p.: Looking Glass Books, 2007.
Forbes. "Chick-fil-A Named America's Favorite Restaurant." www.forbes.com.
Georgia Historical Society "S. Truett Cathy Named Georgia Trustee." www.georgiahistory.com.
WinShape Foundation. www.wikiwand.com.

THOMAS CHATMON

See entry for Mayor Malcolm Maclean (page 116).

GENERAL LUCIUS D. CLAY

DIRECTED THE BERLIN AIRLIFT
APRIL 23, 1897–APRIL 16, 1978

L ucius D. Clay was commander of the U.S. Army in 1948 and helped rebuild Europe after World War II. Clay was born in Marietta to a prominent family that included his father, U.S. senator Alexander Clay.

Lucius graduated from West Point in 1918, earning his commission in the U.S. Army Corps of Engineers. His military duties included building dams and airport facilities and teaching at various army schools, including West Point, later in his career. Clay was close to President Franklin Roosevelt, and during the New Deal programs of the 1930s, he supervised the building of 450 airports all over the United States.

At the beginning of World War II, Clay became the youngest brigadier general in the army. He used his skills as an engineer to direct the construction of and stabilize French harbors, including the harbor at Cherbourg, which was essential to moving war materiel before and during D-Day.

Clay served on General Dwight D. Eisenhower's staff, and after the Germans surrendered in 1945, he became deputy military governor. In 1947, he was promoted to full general of the army and became high commissioner (or military governor) of the American section of occupied Germany. In this role, he oversaw recommendations for rebuilding postwar Germany, which became the basis of the Marshall Plan.

On June 24, 1948, the Soviets, under Stalin's orders, imposed the Berlin Blockade, designed to move American forces out of the city. Clay ordered the Berlin Airlift that defied the Soviets' action by calling for air cargo planes to drop food and medical supplies to U.S. troops and local citizens. It was

General Lucius D. Clay. *Bob Wands/AP/Shutterstock.*

an incredible feat of logistics—at one point, cargo planes landed every four minutes, twenty-four hours a day. The blockade lasted 324 days and was lifted in May 1949 when the Soviets backed down. Under Clay's incredible direction, breaking the blockade was a significant moment of the Cold War and showed American support for the citizens of Berlin.

When Clay returned to America, he was given a ticker-tape parade in New York City. He was put on the cover of *Time* magazine three times and made an honorary citizen of Berlin.

After he retired from military service in 1949, Clay became chairman of the Continental Can Company and later became a partner at Lehman Brothers. He became one of President Eisenhower's closest advisors and an unofficial emissary while Eisenhower was in office. He became the national chairman of Eisenhower's Crusade for Freedom, a propaganda campaign that raised funds for Radio Free Europe and generated support for American Cold War policies. Clay is also considered the principal architect of the national interstate highway system, developed during President Eisenhower's term.

Clay was the father of two sons, both of whom became generals. Dobbins Air Force Base was built in his hometown of Marietta and shares its runways with the General Lucius D. Clay National Guard Center, which opened in 2012. The city named one of its streets Clay Road and a football stadium, Clay Stadium, in his honor.

Sources

Smith, Jean Edward. *Lucius D. Clay: An American Life*. New York: Henry Holt & Co., 1990.
USASOC History Office. "General Lucius D. Clay." usarmy.mil.

PAT CONROY

PRINCE OF TIDES AUTHOR, COURTED CONTROVERSY
OCTOBER 26, 1945–MARCH 4, 2016

P at Conroy was an American author famous for writing books that exposed the racism, violence and hypocrisy of the South. He was born in Atlanta and moved with his U.S. Marine fighter pilot father to military bases around the South. He suffered physical and mental abuse from his father and attended college at The Citadel, a military college located in Charleston, South Carolina.

After graduation, he became a teacher of underprivileged Black children. His school was located on a small island off the South Carolina coast, and Conroy was disheartened by the way the school's administration mistreated the children. He clashed with his boss, and when he took his children on a trick-or-treat trip to white homeowners on the mainland, he was fired by the school's superintendent. Conroy wrote about this experience in the book *The Water Is Wide*, which was made into the motion picture *Conrack* starring Jon Voight.

He moved to Atlanta in 1973 and wrote his next book, *The Great Santini*, which described his childhood living with his abusive father who regularly beat him and his mother. The issue with his father continued to be a part of all future books he published. *The Great Santini* was made into a movie starring Robert Duvall.

His next novel, *The Lords of Discipline*, told of his college life at The Citadel. The book was critical of the college and what Conroy felt was its hypocrisy in mistreating Black and other students during his time there. The president

Pat Conroy. *Lou Krasky/AP/Shutterstock.*

and former students of The Citadel were outraged by his book. Published in 1980, the book was his third novel to be adapted as a movie.

He left Atlanta and moved to Rome, Italy, where he began working on his most famous book, *The Prince of Tides.* The book told of a man's guilt because he abused his wife and children and his healing process that provided a sense of hope and peace. It was published in 1986, and readers loved it, calling the writing a form of poetry. It became a worldwide bestseller, selling millions of copies. *The Prince of Tides* was adapted into a film starring Barbra Streisand and Nick Nolte.

Conroy moved back to South Carolina and Highlands, North Carolina, and continued his writing career, including *Beach Music, My Losing Season,*

South of Broad and other notable novels. In later life, he made peace with his father and wrote *The Death of Santini: The Story of a Father and His Son*. He even made up with others and was honored by The Citadel, giving the college's graduation speech.

His final book, *My Exaggerated Life*, was a story of his early writing days in Atlanta and his friendship with other authors, including Paul Hemphill and Terry Kay, who became famous authors in their own right. On his seventieth birthday, he was celebrated by his friends to honor his extraordinary career. It was his final honor among many other awards he received over his lifetime. He died four months later of pancreatic cancer.

Sources

Conroy, Pat. "My Reading Life." *Deckle Edge*, November 2, 2010.

Grimes, William. "Pat Conroy, Author of 'The Prince of Tides' and 'The Great Santini' Dies at 70." *New York Times*, March 5, 2016.

"Pat Conroy, the Definitive Biography." www.patconroy.com.

TOM GRADY COUSINS

IT'S BETTER TO DO A GOOD DEED, LEFT UNTOLD
DECEMBER 1931-

Tom Cousins is a native of Rome, Georgia, and a well-known and respected real estate developer and philanthropist. He attended and graduated from the University of Georgia in 1952, founding Cousins Properties in 1958. His company was instrumental in changing Atlanta's skyline by developing the CNN Center, the Omni Coliseum and the early phases of the Georgia World Congress Center. Cousins assisted in bringing professional sports franchises to Atlanta, including the National Hockey League's Atlanta Flames and the Atlanta Hawks.

But through his philanthropy, Cousins helped break the cycle of poverty for countless families in Atlanta. With his wife, Ann, Cousins started the East Lake Foundation, created to transform the community of East Lake, a public housing project located about five miles east of downtown Atlanta.

East Lake was also the site of a famous golf course where golf legend Bobby Jones played and started his career. In the 1960s, the surrounding area began to decline, and part of the golf course was sold to developers, who built a large public housing project. The East Lake Meadows housing project became a high-crime, drug-infested area called "Little Vietnam" by local police.

In 1993, Tom Cousins purchased the golf club with plans to restore it, using the renovation as a catalyst to revitalize the surrounding area. The Cousins Foundation then created the East Lake Foundation with $25 million, working through public-private partnerships with the Atlanta Housing Authority, government entities, private foundations and local residents to tear down East Lake's housing project and replace it with a mixed-income apartment block.

Renamed The Villages of East Lake, the site was transformed into a beautiful neighborhood where residents found new opportunities to lift themselves out of poverty. The concept was designed so that middle-income families moved next door to families receiving federal housing assistance. Families saw that their children would grow up in an environment without crime in the streets.

The foundation then created a partnership with the Atlanta Public School system to construct elementary, middle and high schools on the property so that children of low- and middle-

Tom Grady Cousins. *Jennifer Stalcup Photography*.

income families could receive excellent educations. The first school opened in 2000. A few years later, Drew Charter School's test scores became some of the highest in the city, and nearly 100 percent of its first three senior classes graduated and were accepted to college. A new YMCA was built next to the school in 2001 and offered recreational and community programs.

Cousins renovated the 1926 East Lake Golf Club using the original plans and restored the Donald Ross course. In 1998, the club hosted the PGA Tour of Champions, and it became the tournament's permanent home in 2004. The foundation constructed a nine-hole public golf course named for Charlie Yates, with Tiger Woods participating in the grand opening.

Over time, the East Lake community went from having the highest crime rate in Atlanta to having the city's lowest. The East Lake model created national attention as cities looking for ways to transform their neighborhoods adopted similar programs. Together with other visionaries, Cousins created Purpose Built Communities, a national organization that serves as a bridge to connect cities seeking to learn from the East Lake model. The organization helps local city leaders create meaningful change in their neighborhoods. Purpose Built Communities has a presence in communities across the United States, from Florida to New York, from Michigan to Texas.

Tom Cousins has received many awards and honors during his lifetime, but he never wanted to receive personal attention. One friend described him as someone who lives by the adage, "Better than riches, better than gold, is a good deed done and left untold."

Cousins, along with his wife, used his real estate success and influence to make the world a better place to live, and he created a national movement of community revitalization all over America.

Sources

East Lake Foundation. "History." www.eastlakefoundation.org.

Georgia History. "Thomas G. Cousins: Georgia 2012 Georgia Trustee." www.georgiahistory.com.

Percy, Susan. "Tom Cousins: On Role Models, Community Service and Changing Neighborhoods." *Georgia Trend*, January 2012. www.georgiatrend.com.

COACH ROBERT LEE "BOBBY" DODD

BELIEVED THAT FOOTBALL WAS FUN, NOT DRUDGERY
NOVEMBER 11, 1908 –JUNE 21, 1988

B obby Dodd was the most respected and successful coach in Georgia Tech football history. He was born in Virginia and grew up in Tennessee, where he attended college and played football at the University of Tennessee.

He excelled at college football, playing quarterback, tailback and punter. Over three years, he led his team to twenty-seven victories, with only one loss and two ties. The Associated Press selected him as an All-American at tailback.

After graduation, he joined the coaching staff at Georgia Tech. In 1945, he became head coach for the Georgia Tech Yellow Jackets. Dodd's nickname was the "Grey Fox."

Dodd's teams became a powerhouse in an era of great teams and great coaches in the South. Coaches like Bear Bryant at Alabama, Georgia's Wally Butts and Auburn's Ralph "Shug" Jordan were known for brutal practices and hard-nosed football, but Dodd had a different approach. He believed football was fun, not drudgery. He urged his players to spend their time studying and going to church on Sunday. After games, he gave his players the next day off and made his practices short, with little physical contact. Other coaches, like Bryant, wondered how Dodd achieved a winning football program using this approach.

Dodd invented the famous "Belly Series," where the quarterback takes the ball from the center and places it in the belly of the running back, who tries to run up the middle. If the defense tries to tackle the running back, the

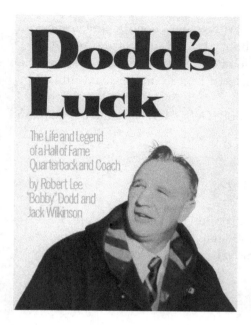

Dodd's Luck

The Life and Legend
of a Hall of Fame
Quarterback and Coach

by Robert Lee
"Bobby" Dodd and
Jack Wilkinson

Dodd's Luck by Robert Lee "Bobby" Dodd and Jack Wilkinson (University of Georgia Press, 1987).

quarterback then takes the ball back and runs it around the end. This offense is still used by teams today. He also used trick plays, including the quick kick, where the Jackets would surprise their opponents by kicking the ball on third down, placing the opponents way behind their goal line. Many times, Tech would cause a fumble, score a touchdown and win the game.

Over twenty-two years, Bobby Dodd's teams had a .713 winning percentage, with a record of 165 wins, only 64 losses and 8 ties. Tech went to 13 bowl games, winning 9, including 8 in a row. Dodd's teams set a school record, winning 31 games in a row against Southeastern Conference teams and teams from other conferences from 1951 to 1953. In 1952, Georgia Tech was undefeated; they beat the University of Mississippi in the 1953 Sugar Bowl and were declared National Champions by the International News Service. For his efforts, Dodd was named Coach of the Year by the *New York Daily News*.

Georgia Tech has a long-standing rivalry with the University of Georgia dating back to 1893. From 1949 to 1956, Tech won eight games in a row against the Bulldogs, outscoring them by 176–39. It is the longest winning series against the two teams and is called "The Drought" by UGA bulldog fans.

After retiring from coaching in 1967, Dodd continued as athletic director until 1976. In 1959, Dodd was elected to the National Football Foundation

College Football Hall of Fame. With other honors, the American Sportsmanship Council created the Bobby Dodd Coach of the Year Award, given for a "style that emphasizes something more than winning the game…a belief that the game of football should be kept in perspective with college life in general."

Two months before his death in 1988, Georgia Tech named its stadium Bobby Dodd Stadium in his honor.

Sources

Cromartie, Bill. *Clean Old-Fashioned Hate*. N.p.: Strode Publishers, Inc., 1977.
Dodd, Robert Lee "Bobby," and Jack Wilkinson. *Dodd's Luck: The Life and Legend of a Hall of Fame Quarterback and Coach*. Savannah, GA: Golden Coast Publishing Co., 1987.

COACH VINCE DOOLEY

GAVE UGA FOOTBALL A NATIONAL CHAMPIONSHIP
SEPTEMBER 4, 1932–

Vince Dooley is regarded as the University of Georgia's greatest football coach. During his twenty-five-season career as head coach (1964–88), he compiled a 201-77-10 record and won 6 Southeastern Conferences (SEC) titles. In 1980, he led the team to win the National Championship and was named NCAA Coach of the Year by several organizations, including the National Sportscasters and Sportswriters Association.

Dooley grew up in Mobile, Alabama, and graduated from Auburn University, where he played quarterback for the Auburn Tigers. He married the former Barbara Meshad and served in the United States Marine Corps. After leaving the military, he returned to Auburn and coached under Ralph "Shug" Jordan.

In 1964, he became head coach at the University of Georgia, and in his first year, he led the Bulldogs to their first winning season in five years. The next season, his Bulldogs beat the top-ranked University of Michigan. The next game, Dooley's Bulldogs beat Coach Bear Bryant's University of Alabama undefeated team on the famous flea-flicker play (the receiver catches the pass and turns and laterals the ball to another player, who races to a winning touchdown). Dooley was off and running, and in 1966, Georgia won the Southeastern Conference.

In 1980, Herschel Walker came to UGA. Walker was a high school running back from Wrightsville, Georgia. In the first game of the season, the Bulldogs were losing to Tennessee, and Dooley decided to put Walker into the game. The young freshman ran all over Tennessee. On one play, Walker

Coach Vince Dooley. *Jennifer Stalcup Photography.*

went through the line and ran over three players for a touchdown. For the balance of the year, with Walker's leadership, Georgia was undefeated and won the national championship against Notre Dame.

Over the twenty-five years Dooley coached Georgia, he had only one losing season, and in one span from 1980 to 1984, his teams won forty-three games, lost only four and tied one. He won many awards, including National Football Coach of the Year in 1980. He was inducted into the Georgia Sports Hall of Fame and the National College Football of Fame.

In 1988, Dooley retired as Georgia's football coach and became the university's full-time athletic director (a position he had held since 1979). During his tenure, the athletic programs in multiple sports—including women's gymnastics, swimming, men's tennis and men's golf—won championships. Overall, his teams won seventy-eight SEC championships plus several national championships. In 2004, the National Association of Collegiate Directors of Athletics (NACDA) presented him with the James J. Corbett Memorial Award for his devotion to intercollegiate athletics.

After his retirement from UGA in 2004, Dooley launched another career as an author, gardener, public speaker and historian. He wrote many books, including *Vince Dooley's Garden*, *A History of the University of Georgia*, a children's book about Georgia's Bulldog mascot and many books about Georgia football.

Dooley is a member of the Georgia Historical Society and has served as its chairman. He works with the Salvation Army and other civic and community nonprofits. He was named a Georgia Trustee, the state's highest honor, in 2011.

Dooley's wife, Barbara, is a public speaker and hosts a radio show. Both appear together as keynote speakers, entertaining people at conventions and community events all over the state. In 2019, Georgia's Board of Regents honored Dooley by naming the field at Sanford Stadium Dooley Field.

Sources

Cromartie, Bill. *Clean Old-Fashioned Hate*. N.p.: Strode Publishers, Inc., 1977.

Dooley, Vince, with Tony Barnhart. *Dooley: My 40 Years at Georgia*. Chicago: Triumph Books, 2005.

Nelson, Jon. *College Football at UGA*. Charleston, SC: The History Press, 2012.

Smith, Loran, with Lewis Grizzard. *Glory! Glory! Glory!* Atlanta: Peachtree Publishers Ltd., 1981.

W.E.B. DU BOIS

AFRICAN AMERICAN CIVIL RIGHTS ACTIVIST,
FOUNDER OF THE NAACP
FEBRUARY 23, 1868–AUGUST 27, 1963

Du Bois was a civil rights leader born in Massachusetts. He attended Fisk University in Nashville, Tennessee, and became the first Black American to earn a PhD from Harvard University. He served as a history and economics professor at Atlanta University (now Clark Atlanta University) and later became chairman of the department of sociology at the school.

Du Bois was an influential leader and voice for Black rights in the first part of the twentieth century in a world dominated by whites. In 1905, he founded the Niagara Movement, made up of Black scholars and professionals. In 1909, he was one of the founders of the National Association for the Advancement of Colored People (NAACP) and was editor of the *Crisis*, its monthly magazine.

During his leadership of the *Crisis* magazine, he focused on gaining equal treatment for Black people as granted by the U.S. Constitution's Fourteenth Amendment. He protested white supremacist ideas that Black citizens were inferior. He wrote bitter editorials against white Americans, and the magazine became the leading protest publication of its day.

Du Bois was a prolific scholar. His dissertation at Harvard was titled "The Suppression of the African Slave Trade to the United States of America, 1638–1870." A pioneering study named "The Philadelphia Negro: A Social Study" assured his place among leading scholars.

W.E.B. Du Bois. *Library of Congress.*

While at Atlanta University, he organized conferences titled "Studies of the Negro Problem." He edited or co-edited annual publications on topics including "The Negro in Business," "The Negro Artisan," "The Negro Church" and "The Negro American Family," one of the best collections of papers on Black American history during this time. He wrote a book about John Brown that was a sympathetic portrayal of the American abolitionist who believed in armed revolution as the best way to overthrow the institution of slavery in 1856.

Du Bois organized a Pan-African Congress that advocated a movement to free African colonies from European powers. The Pan-African Congress encouraged and strengthened bonds of solidarity between people of African descent.

Du Bois became the voice for his race and inspiration for all Americans who believed in integrating people of color into American society. He lived to see the 1954 U.S. Supreme Court ruling in *Brown v. the Board of Education* that overturned laws in southern states segregating schools by race. On August 27, 1963, he died at age ninety-five, just one day before Dr. Martin Luther King delivered his "I Have a Dream" speech at the March on Washington.

Source

Lewis, David Levering. *W.E.B. Du Bois, 1868–1919: Biography of a Race.* New York: Henry Holt and Company, 1993.

REBECCA ANN LATIMER FELTON

THE FIRST WOMAN SEATED IN THE U.S. SENATE
JUNE 10, 1835–JANUARY 24, 1930

B orn in Decatur, Rebecca Ann Felton attended Madison Female College and graduated first in her class. In 1852, she married William H. Felton, who shared her politics advocating temperance and women's rights. When her husband won a seat in the U.S. Congress, she assisted him in planning campaign strategy, writing speeches and drafting legislation.

She became a significant political force in Georgia when she joined the *Atlanta Journal* as a columnist and advocate for the national temperance movement. She supported passage of the Eighteenth Amendment, and she used the backing of local churches and others to pass local Prohibition laws. Prohibition was a nationwide constitutional ban on the production, importation, transportation and sale of alcoholic beverages from 1920 to 1933.

Felton also achieved stature as a speaker for equal rights for women. She worked for white women's right to vote, to receive free public education and admittance into public universities. She encouraged the Georgia legislature to pass the Suffrage Bill, allowing women to vote in the 1920 presidential election. Though her bill went down in defeat, women earned the right to vote in Georgia in 1922.

She criticized southern men who boasted of their superior chivalry toward women while opposing white women's right to vote. But Felton was a white supremacist. In her columns and speeches, she called Blacks half-gorillas with a brutal lust for white women. She advocated the lynching of Black men and promoted the idea that white southerners should engage in large movements to lynch Blacks to protect society.

In 1922, Georgia governor Thomas Hardwick appointed her to fill the Senate seat left vacant by Tom Watson's death. Walter George defeated her in a special election. However, as a sign of respect for Felton's age (eighty-seven) and her status in the national suffrage movement, George didn't immediately take his seat when the Senate reconvened. Felton was sworn in as the first woman senator in U.S. history, though technically she never served. George took office the next day.

Senator Rebecca Felton. *Library of Congress.*

Felton retired to her home in Cartersville and finished her last book, *The Romantic Story of Georgia's Women*. She died in 1930, after more than five decades of fighting for women's suffrage.

Source

Felton, Mrs. William H. *My Memoirs of Georgia Politics*. Atlanta: Index Printing Company, 1911. Repr., Nablus Public Domain Reprints.

SENATOR WALTER F. GEORGE

HE SERVED DURING TWO WORLD WARS
JANUARY 29, 1878–AUGUST 4, 1957

George was an important leader in the Senate during World War I and World II. He served on the Committee on Foreign Relations (1940–41), and following World War II, he was president pro tempore of the Senate. He was elected in 1922 and served in that role for thirty-five years. Senator Walter George and Senator Richard Russell were called two of the most important Congress members from a single state.

George was born on a farm in South Georgia, where his parents were sharecroppers. He attended Mercer University, graduating from law school in 1900. George set up his law practice in Vienna, Georgia, and became a superior judge in the local community. He became a member of the Georgia Court of Appeals and later associate justice of the Supreme Court of Georgia.

George was elected as a Democrat to the U.S. Senate in 1922 after Senator Thomas E. Watson's death. He was reelected in 1926, 1932, 1938, 1944 and 1950 before resigning in 1958 to serve as President Dwight Eisenhower's special ambassador to the North Atlantic Treaty Organization (NATO).

The Great Depression in the 1930s was hard on Georgia, and George supported programs beneficial to the state, including forming the Tennessee Valley Authority and the Agricultural Adjustment Act, passed to help farmers by increasing crop prices.

During President Franklin D. Roosevelt's second term, George opposed the president's attempt to pack the U.S. Supreme Court with more justices who would support his New Deal policies. Roosevelt encouraged a man to run against George in the election of 1941, but the effort failed, and George won reelection in a landslide.

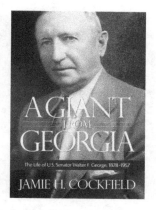

Senator Walter F. George.
Mercer University Press.

George and Roosevelt mended their political fences, and the senator frequently supported Roosevelt, including the decision to declare war on Japan and Germany during World War II. He was chairman of the Senate Foreign Relations Committee and the Senate Finance Committee, and he gave enthusiastic support for the war effort.

In the 1950s, George was a supporter of Republican president Dwight D. Eisenhower. He was a good friend of Secretary of State John Foster Dulles and worked to support American foreign policy during the Cold War. His bipartisan support won acclaim from his fellow congressmen on both sides of the aisle.

Sources

Cackfield, Jamie H. *A Giant from Georgia: The Life of U.S. Senator Walter F. George, 1878–1957*. Macon, GA: Mercer University Press, 2019.

Senator Walter George, Papers. Collection number RBRL/204/WFG, University of Georgia. russelldoc.galib.edu.

"U.S. Senate, Walter George." www.senate.gov.

MARVIN GRIFFIN

See entry for Lester Maddox (page 120).

GOVERNOR JOE FRANK HARRIS

REFORMED GEORGIA'S PUBLIC SCHOOL SYSTEM
FEBRUARY 16, 1936–

J oe Frank Harris is the father of the Quality-Based Education Act (QBE), designed to improve the quality of education for high school students and increase student achievement throughout Georgia. At the time of its passage in 1985, Georgia was ranked near the bottom of the fifty states in education, teacher salaries and educational resources. Thanks to his reforms, Georgia schools more than doubled that ranking over his eight years in office.

Harris was born and grew up in Cartersville and graduated from the University of Georgia in 1958. After graduation, he joined the family business, Harris Cement Products.

He ran for the Georgia House of Representatives and served eighteen years before being elected governor in 1982. Harris served two terms from 1982 to 1991, presiding over a period of tremendous growth in the state. More than 850,000 jobs were created as the state's population grew from five million to almost eight million over twenty years.

Harris's legislative triumph occurred in 1985, when QBE passed. Before the passage of QBE, schools received funding from the state based on the number of students enrolled. This formula penalized small rural counties without the tax base to support education funding in their county. Harris's new formula provided funding for schools based on the number of hours students were in class during a school day. Harris also gave additional money to counties that increased local taxes to support their schools. The legislation increased salaries for educators, established merit pay incentives

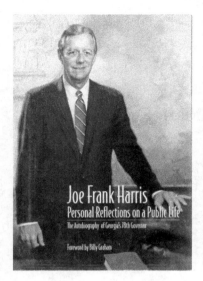

Governor Joe Frank Harris. *Mercer University Press.*

for outstanding teachers and funded continuing-education opportunities to encourage advanced college degrees for teachers. One of QBE's goals was to reduce student-teacher ratios to create smaller class sizes and establish standard ways to measure results in math, science, language and health taught in each school. Harris's program encouraged Head Start and full-day kindergarten programs for schools and a Quality Core Curriculum (QCC), standardized guidelines for specific material to be taught at every grade level.

His administration raised awareness of drug abuse and adult illiteracy, and he introduced projects to protect the environment. His two terms helped lay the foundation for Georgia to become a leader in economic development in the country. Harris built more libraries in Georgia than any other governor and ended his term in office by winning the 1989 National Distinguished Leadership Award from the American Planning Association.

On his retirement, Harris moved back to Cartersville and wrote his memoir, *Personal Reflections on a Public Life.* In 1992, he served on the Board of Regents for the University System of Georgia, and he continues to serve on several charities.

Sources

Harris, Joe Frank. *Personal Reflections on a Public Life.* Cartersville, GA: Etowah Valley Historical Society, n.d.

National Governor Association. "Joe Frank Harris." www.NAG.org.

New Georgia Encyclopedia. "Quality Basic Education." www.georgiaencyclopedia.org.

JOEL CHANDLER HARRIS

WROTE FAMOUS UNCLE REMUS STORIES
DECEMBER 9, 1845–JULY 3, 1908

H arris was a writer of folklorist books and was known for his collection of Uncle Remus stories. He was born in Eatonton, and as a young man, he served as a printer devil for a local newspaper, *The Countryman*, which was published on Turnwold Plantation. Joseph Addison Turner, the plantation owner, was his mentor, teaching him to write stories and publishing his weekly columns.

Harris got an exemption from serving in the Civil War because of his slight build and because he worked for a newspaper loyal to the Southern cause, which aided the Confederate war effort. During the war years, he became friends with local Black people who lived on the plantations around Eatonton. He learned colorful folk stories from those enslaved on the plantation, including Uncle George Terrell, Old Harbert and Aunt Crissy. They told him stories of animals such as foxes, rabbits, bears and other forest animals that survived by fooling others into ridiculous situations.

After the war, Harris worked at several newspapers in Georgia and eventually landed a job as a column writer with the *Atlanta Constitution*. Harris started repeating these stories using the same dialect used by the two friends. These columns were called "Tales of Uncle Remus: The Adventures of Brer Rabbit." The columns were popular and reprinted in many newspapers across the country. Harris's stories soon made him famous.

In 1880, Harris compiled a book of his columns called *Uncle Remus: His Songs and His Sayings*, illustrated by artist A.B. Frost. The book sold thousands of copies all over America. It has since been translated into more than thirty

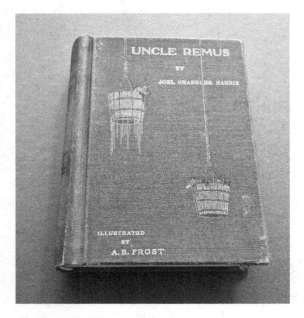

Uncle Remus, by Joel Chandler Harris. *From Neely Young's collection, photo by Heidi Rizzi.*

languages and sold all over the world. It was revised and reprinted in 1895 and 1908, becoming one of the most popular books of the era and making Harris famous.

After he died in 1908, the stories continued to be read and published. In 1946, movie producer Walt Disney made a musical film based on the collection of Uncle Remus stories. *The Song of the South* was a live action/animated film using Brer Rabbit, Brer Fox and others telling the tales made famous in the *Uncle Remus* book. The movie was a success, and one of its songs, "Zip-a-Dee-Doo-Dah," won the 1947 Academy Award for Best Original Song. James Baskett received an Honorary Academy Award for his performance as Uncle Remus.

Later, the movie became controversial. The stories depicted enslaved people being happy with their servitude to white plantation owners before and during the Civil War in 1864. Many of the stories portrayed Black people as inferior, and the book pictured plantation life as idyllic. Both Blacks and whites criticized the Black vernacular as offensive; Disney eventually pulled the movie off the shelf and refused to allow additional copies to be produced.

The Uncle Remus character is a product of the attitude of whites during Harris's time. The book and movie and Harris himself became vilified as racist, though some of the charges are untrue. In his columns in the

Atlanta Constitution in the early part of the century, Harris deplored violence against Black people and insisted that the two races should live side by side peacefully. His son and daughter-in-law, Julian and Julia Harris, were journalists and, in the 1920s, openly attacked the Ku Klux Klan in their editorials, winning a Pulitzer Prize for their efforts.

Sources

Harris, Joel Chandler. *On the Plantation: A Story of a Georgia Boy's Adventures during the War*. Foreword by Erskine Caldwell. New York: D. Appleton and Company, 1982. Repr., Athens: Brown Thrasher Books, University of Georgia Press, 1980.
———. *Uncle Remus: His Songs and His Sayings*. New York: D. Appleton and Company, 1914.

JULIAN AND JULIA COLLIER HARRIS

GEORGIA'S FIRST PULITZER PRIZE WINNERS
JULIAN: JUNE 21, 1874–FEBRUARY 9, 1963
JULIA: NOVEMBER 11, 1875–JANUARY 21, 1967

Julian and Julia Harris were publishers and editors of the *Columbus Enquirer-Sun* in Columbus, Georgia. Their newspaper published stories that aroused public indignation over Ku Klux Klan activity, and the Harrises received the 1926 Pulitzer Prize for their fearless journalism.

The couple were both born in Georgia and married in 1897. After college, they worked as journalists at the *Atlanta Journal* and then at the *New York Herald*. In 1920, they came to Columbus, Georgia, and bought the *Columbus Enquirer-Sun*. They used their newspaper to crusade for social progress and took on the KKK. The Klan was a secret organization, but the Harrises exposed them by publishing members' names. They wrote editorials asking for justice for Black people and condemned the practice of lynching (the killing of an alleged offender by mob action without a trial).

They put their lives at risk when the Klan tried to stop their editorials by burning crosses in front of their home and business. They wrote and published editorials demanding dishonest, racist and incompetent public officials resign their offices. The Harrises wrote stories condemning other laws, including one that barred the teaching of evolution in schools. Their influence spread to other southern newspapers, and many took up their cause for social justice.

In 1926, Julian and Julia Harris, and their publication, were awarded the Pulitzer Prize for public service. The award cited the Harrises and the newspaper for "their brave and energetic fight against the Ku Klux Klan; against the enactment of a law barring the teaching of evolution; against

Left: Julia Collier Harris. *Right*: Julian Harris. *Library of Congress.*

dishonest and incompetent public officials and for justice to the Negro and against lynching."

Eventually, the battle became too much. They were writing about controversial subjects for a small town in the South, and the Klan soon pressured advertisers to stop placings ads in the *Enquirer*. As a result, they lost their newspaper in 1929 and had to move back to Atlanta. Julia published a book on Julian's famous father, *Joel Chandler Harris: Editor and Essayist*, the following year, and Julian eventually became the southern correspondent for the *New York Times* in 1942.

Sources

Georgia Writers Hall of Fame. "Julian and Julia Harris." georgiawritershalloffame.org.

Harris, Julia Collier. *The Life and Letters of Joel Chandler Harris.* New York: AMS Press, 1918.

Libby, George. "Julian Harris and the *Columbus Enquirer-Sun*: Consequences of Winning the Pulitzer Prize." Academia, April 1988. www.academia.edu.

MAYOR WILLIAM B. HARTSFIELD

HELPED DEVELOP ATLANTA INTO AN AVIATION HUB
MARCH 1, 1890–FEBRUARY 22, 1971

C alled the greatest mayor of Atlanta, William Hartsfield served as mayor longer than any person, six terms, from 1937 to 1941 and 1942 until 1961. He was born in Atlanta and stayed in the city all his life.

He became a law clerk at former governor John Slaton's firm, Rosser, Slaton, Phillips, and Hopkins, and was admitted to the Georgia Bar in 1917. He entered politics in 1922 as an Atlanta City Council member and was elected mayor in 1936. He is credited with building the Atlanta–Fulton County Airport and growing it from a small municipal facility in 1925 to one of the largest airports in the United States. He held office when metro Atlanta grew from 100,000 people to more than 1 million inhabitants.

Hartsfield gained national attention when he advocated a practical approach to the civil rights movement during the turbulent desegregation period after World War II and during the 1950s and 1960s. He helped negotiate as Atlanta's white business leaders and African American leaders integrated their businesses. In 1953, Martin Luther King Sr. campaigned for Hartsfield and led the Black community's support for his election. When Martin Luther King Jr. was arrested at a sit-in in Atlanta in 1960, Hartsfield saw that the charges were dropped. He led the effort to merge Atlanta's white and Black high schools when other southern cities were fighting to keep the races separate. He helped Atlanta earn its reputation as the "City Too Busy to Hate."

During the period he served as mayor, Hartsfield took the city from nearly declaring bankruptcy during the Great Depression to a $3.5 million

WILLIAM BERRY
HARTSFIELD
MAYOR OF ATLANTA

BY HAROLD H. MARTIN

William Berry Hartsfield: Mayor of Atlanta, by Harold H. Martin (University of Georgia Press, 1978).

budget surplus. He created a Department of Public Safety to merge the city's police, fire and traffic departments. He was a staunch critic of the state's county unit system, which favored rural counties and diminished the voice of Black voters, until it was struck down by the U.S. Supreme Court in 1962. To provide Atlanta with an abundant water supply, he supported building Buford Dam on the Chattahoochee River.

As a city alderman, and later as mayor, Hartsfield convinced leaders to purchase an abandoned racetrack south of the city. In 1925, Mayor Walter Sims signed a lease with the idea of it being an airfield. Hartsfield was the first commissioner to sign the agreement, steering the airport from the barnstorming era to the jet age. He helped bring Delta Air Lines to the city—its primary hub is in Atlanta— and over the years, the airport expanded so that it now covers more than 4,700 acres and serves more than 104 million passengers annually. It's been named the busiest airport in the world for twenty-two consecutive years.

Hartsfield made many significant and lasting contributions to the city of Atlanta. A week after his death, the Atlanta City Council renamed the airport Hartsfield Atlanta International Airport (now Hartsfield-Jackson Atlanta International Airport) in his honor.

Sources

Hartsfield, William Berry. Papers, circa 1960s–1893. Emory Libraries, collection number 558. www.emory.edu,

Martin, Harold H. *William Berry Hartsfield: Mayor of Atlanta*. Athens: University of Georgia Press, 1978.

ALONZO FRANKLIN HERNDON
AND NORRIS B. HERNDON

FOUNDERS OF THE MOST SUCCESSFUL
BLACK-OWNED BUSINESS IN AMERICA
ALONZO: JUNE 26, 1858–JULY 21, 1927
NORRIS: JULY 15, 1897–JUNE 15, 1977

Alonzo Herndon was the founder of the Atlanta Life Insurance Company, which sought to build confidence in Black entrepreneurs and create jobs for African Americans during the Jim Crow era. Herndon was an inspiration to others, and through his actions, he grew his company into the most successful Black-owned business in America, making him Atlanta's first Black millionaire.

Herndon was born into slavery. His father was a white slave owner, Frank Herndon, who owned Herndon's mother, Sophenie, and did not acknowledge his two sons. They lived on a farm in Social Circle. He was emancipated at age seven at the end of the Civil War and sent from the farm with his mother, brother and maternal grandparents. They were impoverished and homeless, but they were free. Herndon worked as a laborer and a peddler to help the family make ends meet.

As a young man, he was a good student. With little formal education, he joined a barbershop in Jonesboro, Georgia. In 1882, Herndon moved to Atlanta and worked for the local barber, William Hutchins. He eventually opened his own shops, including one on Peachtree Street known as the Crystal Palace, and it became the best barbershop in Atlanta, catering to Black businessmen and white lawyers, judges, politicians and businessmen. His business prospered, and he invested in real estate, owned more than one hundred rental houses and purchased an estate near Tavares, Florida.

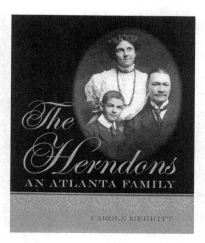

The Herndons: An Atlanta Family, by Carole Merritt (University of Georgia Press, 2002).

In 1905, Herndon purchased a failing insurance company that had only $5,000 in assets. He named the enterprise the Atlanta Mutual Insurance Association and grew the company so that it soon held more than $400,000 in assets. In 1922, the company reorganized as the Atlanta Life Insurance Company. He merged with other insurance companies and expanded his operations into Florida, Kansas, Kentucky, Missouri, Tennessee and Texas.

He was active in political and economic efforts and was a founding member of the National Negro Business League. His friends included Booker T. Washington and W.E.B. Du Bois. His business success enabled him to support other local Atlanta causes, including the Young Men's Christian Association (YMCA), Atlanta University and other organizations, such as a kindergarten for Black children. He helped start the Atlanta State Saving Bank that supported Black-owned businesses and Black families during challenging economic times. He was an investor in the first Black-owned drugstore on Auburn Avenue.

He was married to Adrienne McNeil, a professor at Atlanta University, and had one son, Norris. After she passed away in 1910, he married Jessie Gillespie, who, along with his son, became an important partner in the company. He and Jessie built a home that, at one time, was one of the largest mansions in Atlanta. In 2000, Herndon Home was designated a National Historic Landmark.

After Herndon's death in Atlanta at age sixty-nine, his son, Norris B. Herndon, continued his father's legacy. For the next fifty years, Norris guided Atlanta Life to even greater success. As the company's president, he amassed a fortune estimated at more than $100 million. He played a significant role during the civil rights movement by providing funding to Martin Luther King Jr. and other leaders in the fight for equality for Black people and people of color. Norris died on June 15, 1977. He personified the ambitions and dreams by which his father lived and aspired to—humility, hard work, success and philanthropy.

Sources

African American Registry. "Alonzo Herndon, Pioneering Businessman."
   aaregistry.com.
Merritt, Carole. *The Herndons: An Atlanta Family*. Athens: University of Georgia
   Press, 2002.
VanHouten, Matt. "Alonzo Franklin Herndon (1858–1927 bio)." Black Past,
   January 6, 2011. blackpast.org.

GENERAL COURTNEY HICKS HODGES

HE WENT FROM PRIVATE TO FOUR-STAR GENERAL
JANUARY 5, 1897–JANUARY 16, 1966

General Courtney Hicks Hodges was a military officer who led the First Army in World War II. Born in Perry, his father was the publisher and editor of the local newspaper, the *Perry News*. He received an appointment to West Point but stayed only one year before entering the U.S. Army as a private. When he earned his fourth star in 1945, Hodges was one of only two soldiers at the time to go from private to four-star general. (There have since been several more.) He never sought attention, and his friends often remarked that he looked more like a schoolteacher than a general.

During World I, Hicks led the army in an attack against German forces across the Marne River and received the Distinguished Service Cross for his efforts. After the war, he was asked to be an instructor at West Point even though he never graduated from the institution, and in 1940, he became commandant of the Infantry School at Fort Benning.

In 1941, he was promoted to the rank of major general. After America entered the war against Germany, he commanded the Third Army and served under General Omar Bradley during D-Day. In 1944, he succeeded Bradley and took command of the First Army troops that were the first to reach Paris, France, on August 25.

Hodges's First Army troops played a significant role in the Battle of the Bulge, the German army's last effort to turn the tide against American forces. He led his soldiers and joined up with General Patton's troops in a pincer-like movement to cross the Rhine River into Nazi Germany. He kept up the attack and crossed the Elbe River to meet the Soviet army.

General Courtney
Hicks Hodges (*left*).
Atlanta History Center.

After the German surrender, Hodges was ordered to take his army to the Pacific to prepare for the invasion of Japan, but that became unnecessary when Japan surrendered, a result of the devastating atomic bomb attacks on Hiroshima and Nagasaki. His involvement made him present at the surrenders of both Germany and Japan.

General Omar Bradley said of Hicks, "He successfully blended dexterity and common sense in such equal proportions as to produce a magnificently balanced command." When he retired, his hometown of Perry created a museum to honor him and his service to his country. Senator Sam Nunn praised Hodges by saying, "He is remembered as one of the most accomplished battlefield leaders America has produced."

In his speech to the citizens of Perry, Hicks asked that honors bestowed on him be focused instead on "those who are still fighting overseas, to those who will never return and to those who stand ready to finish the job in the world." Nunn said, "Courtney Hicks Hodge always deflected credit to the fighting man."

Hodges retired in 1949 and moved to San Antonio, Texas, and he died in 1996. He once said, "I love the American soldier....He is my work. And I don't think he has any equals."

Sources

"Courtney Hicks Hodges." theworldsmilitaryhistory.wiki.org.
New York Times. "General Courtney Hodges, 79, Dies." January 17, 1966, 38.

HAMILTON HOLMES
AND CHARLAYNE HUNTER-GAULT

REMARKABLE HEROISM
IN THE FACE OF HISTORICAL CHANGE
HOLMES: JULY 8, 1941–OCTOBER 26, 1995
HUNTER-GAULT: FEBRUARY 27, 1942–

C harlayne Hunter-Gault and Hamilton Holmes broke the color barrier at the University of Georgia. They were the first people of color to enroll in the college in the twentieth century. It was a historic event because in the past, Black students were denied admittance.

On January 6, 1961, Federal Judge William Bootle ordered the university to admit the two students, stating, "They would have already been admitted had it not been for their race and color." Hunter (her last name prior to her marriage) and Holmes enrolled and started regular classes.

Things didn't go smoothly when an angry mob gathered outside Hunter's dormitory, protesting her admission. The group caused property damage and considerable distress for Hunter and Holmes. Governor Ernest Vandiver had Hunter and Holmes removed and then waited a few days before returning them to school with police protection.

Other states in the South refused to allow Black students to attend their public colleges. Vandiver also campaigned on a platform to maintain the status quo of segregated schools. He promised to close every school if even "one Negro" entered a white school. But the governor reversed his position and followed the judge's order, and he and state officials condemned the rioters. In coming to the state's top college, Hunter and Holmes demonstrated tremendous courage and paved the way for the peaceful integration of other public schools and colleges in Georgia.

They often felt isolated from other students on campus, though some white students accepted them. One group of students wanted to make sure

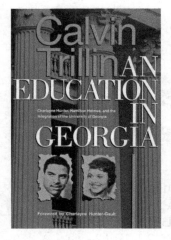

An Education in Georgia, by Calvin Trillin (University of Georgia Press, 1964).

they would be safe when they walked to their classes. A white student organized a group to shadow Holmes and Hunter by walking twenty yards ahead and twenty yards behind them to make sure the two would be safe.

The college's dean of student affairs, William Tate, made sure they had no trouble on campus. The university remained open, with students and teachers keeping classrooms and dorms open as usual. Soon after, the Georgia legislature confirmed Judge Bootle's order. Holmes's and Hunter's willingness to endure to the end makes their heroism even more remarkable.

Charlayne Hunter was born in South Carolina to Charles and Althea Hunter. Her father was a chaplain in the U.S. Army, and she grew up living on military installations across the country until high school, when she moved to Atlanta. She graduated from Henry McNeal Turner High School in Atlanta in 1960. She was rejected when she first applied to UGA. Hunter then enrolled at Wayne State University in Detroit.

The NAACP Legal Defense Fund and some Atlanta attorneys encouraged her to reapply to UGA to help jump-start the university's integration process. She reapplied and was admitted in January 1961. She graduated with a BA in journalism in 1963.

Hunter-Gault soon accepted a job with the *New Yorker* magazine. She later moved to television and became evening anchor for a Washington, D.C. television station. She returned to print journalism in 1968, writing for the *New York Times*.

In 1978, she joined the *MacNeil/Lehrer NewsHour* on PBS as a national correspondent and later joined NPR as a chief correspondent in Africa. In 1999, she joined CNN as the Johannesburg, South Africa bureau chief. She has won many journalism awards, including two George Foster Peabody and National News awards. Today, Hunter-Gault lives in South Africa with her husband, banker Ron Gault.

Hamilton Holmes was born in Atlanta and also attended Atlanta's Henry McNeal Turner High School, graduating in 1959 as valedictorian. He graduated from UGA in 1963. While at the university, he was elected to Phi Beta Kappa and Phi Kappa Phi honor societies.

After graduating from the University of Georgia, Holmes became the first Black student enrolled at Emory University School of Medicine. He became a member of Emory's faculty as an assistant professor of orthopedics. He served as chief of orthopedics at the Veterans Administration hospital in Atlanta and ended his career as the head of orthopedic surgery at Grady Hospital in Atlanta.

The University of Georgia established the annual Holmes-Hunter Lecture Series, and Holmes and Hunter-Gault established an academic scholarship for African American students attending UGA in 1992. In 2001, the university renamed the school's academic building Holmes-Hunter Academic Building in their honor for demonstrating heroism in the face of historical change.

Sources

The Historymaker. "Charlayne Hunter-Gault Biography." www.thehistorymaker.org.

Hunter-Gault, Charlayne. *In My Place*. New York: Vintage Books, 1993.

———. *To the Mountain Top: My Journey Through the Civil Rights Movement*. New York; Roaring Brook Press, n.d.

Marietta Daily Journal. "Bill Dunaway, Witnessing the Desegregation of UGA." February 17, 2021, A-3. www.mdjonline.com.

Nash, Amanda. "Hamilton Holmes." New Georgia Encyclopedia, August 19, 2005. georgiaencyclopedia.org.

Skyer, Heather. "UGA Celebration 60 Years of Desegregation." Online Athens, December 16, 2020. onlineathens.com.

Trillin, Calvin. *An Education in Georgia: Charlayne Hunter, Holmes, and the Integration of the University of Georgia*. Athens: University of Georgia Press, 1992.

MAYOR MAYNARD H. JACKSON

THE FIRST BLACK MAYOR OF ATLANTA
MARCH 23, 1938–JUNE 23, 2003

C alled the Founding Father of the New Atlanta, Maynard Jackson was the first Black mayor of Atlanta. He was from a prominent family; his father was a Baptist preacher, and his mother was a professor and daughter of John Wesley Dobbs, a Black civic leader from the early twentieth century. Jackson graduated from Morehouse College at the age of eighteen and earned his law degree from North Carolina Central University in 1964.

He was only thirty-five years old when he won his first mayoral election in 1973, and during his three terms (1974–82 and 1990–94), Jackson helped turn Atlanta's airport into the largest in the country. He increased the number of minority contractors doing business with the city, prepared the city to host the 1996 Olympic Games and helped the city become a mecca for Black business and culture.

Standing six feet, four inches tall, Jackson cut an intimidating figure. In his early years as mayor, he sparred with the city's white elite leaders. He sometimes bitterly fought with the state's powerful political structure, even staring down the governor and others to gain airport contracts for minorities. Later in his second term, Jackson earned the confidence of Atlanta's business leadership and built bridges that spanned economic, racial and class lines.

He instituted the "joint-venture program," bringing together white-owned and minority-owned firms, elevating the percentage of city contracts awarded to minorities from less than 1 percent in 1973 to 38.6 percent just five years later. Under his watch, the joint-venture program produced almost twenty-five new Black millionaires.

Maynard H. Jackson. *Atlanta History Center.*

In the late 1970s, Jackson campaigned to expand Hartsfield International Airport. The airport was in the middle of the pack for airports in the United States. By adding additional hangars and remodeling and increasing the main terminal's size, Jackson helped the airport's largest tenant, Delta Air Lines, expand its business to become a worldwide company with flights to every major city in the world. Other carriers were attracted to the expanded facility, and by the end of Jackson's third term, Hartsfield International Airport had the largest number of passenger-booked flights in the United States.

A young attorney named Billy Payne approached Andrew Young, the civil rights activist and former mayor, and Jackson with the idea of Atlanta making a bid to win the 1996 Olympic Games. The three traveled to Cuba and made a successful case to the International Olympic Committee. They presented Atlanta as a city that overcame racial tensions and regional poverty to become a global city. Atlanta was chosen for the 1996 Summer Olympics at the Ninety-Sixth Olympic Committee Session in Tokyo, Japan, on August 18, 1990.

The 1996 Games had an enormous impact on the city. Buildings, venues and stadiums were constructed in Atlanta and throughout the metro area to host sporting events and other Olympic-related events. Centennial Olympic Stadium (which was retrofitted and became Turner Field, now Georgia State University's Center Parc Stadium) and Centennial Olympic Park located in the center of the city greatly impacted the local economy, bringing in more than $5 billion in revenue.

Many offices, hotels and other facilities were built around the park, making the city profitable, vibrant and exciting. The Olympics provided a way to give Atlanta and Georgia new energy, revitalize neglected neighborhoods and boost the economy.

During his second term, Jackson faced a painful period when twenty-nine young Black children and men were kidnapped and murdered as part of the notorious Atlanta child murders. The case brought national attention, and Jackson put extra pressure on the police and himself to catch the perpetrator. Finally, a small-time music producer named Wayne Williams was seen throwing a child's body into the Chattahoochee River close to Atlanta. Williams was charged with and convicted of two of the killings and sent to life in prison.

Jackson ran for a third term, and his political career spanned a quarter-century. In his third term, he expanded his efforts by giving a voice to inner-city neighborhoods, establishing a cultural affairs department and creating a new city charter.

After undergoing heart bypass surgery in 1992, Jackson decided not to run for a fourth term in 1993. He finished his term, helping with the multimillion-dollar preparations for the 1996 Olympic Games and helping host the Games.

Jackson died in 2003 and is buried at historic Oakland Cemetery in Atlanta. After his death, the city and mayor changed the Atlanta airport's name to Hartfield-Jackson Atlanta International Airport in his honor.

Sources

Allen, Frederick. *Atlanta Rising*. Atlanta: Longstreet Press, 1996.

Pomerantz, Gary M. *Where Peachtree Meets Sweet Auburn*. New York: Penguin Books, 1996.

Rice, Bradley. "Maynard Jackson, 1938–2003." New Georgia Encyclopedia, July 28, 2004. www.georgiaencyclopedia.org.

HERBERT JENKINS

See entry for Mayor Malcolm Maclean (page 116).

JESSE JEWELL AND GEORGE L. CAGLE

TWO WHO BROUGHT CHICKEN TO THE WORLD
JEWELL: MARCH 13, 1902–JANUARY 16, 1975
CAGLE: 1899–OCTOBER 12, 1982

In 1920, Jesse Jewell and George Cagle joined forces to make the small city of Gainesville the "Poultry Capital of the World." Jewell and Cagle helped create a sector that became the backbone of Georgia's largest industry: agribusiness.

Jewell converted a small feed and seed store into a chicken house. He bought baby chicks and gave them to farmers to raise, then provided credit and sold feed to the farmers to bring the chicks to adulthood. Jewell then repurchased the chickens and sold them to retail consumers.

In 1940, he started a hatchery, followed by a processing plant, feed mill and rendering plant by 1954. It was the first vertically integrated concept where all facets of the process were held within one company.

Jewell helped farmers start their own companies, and the poultry industry took off. They supplied processed chicken products to major grocery stores all over the United States. By the 1950s and 1960s, poultry had become 50 percent of Georgia's economy.

Jewell was a founder of the National Broiler Council and was its first president. His financial success enabled him to give to many nonprofits, including a scholarship fund at nearby Brenau College.

In the 1940s, George Cagle opened a small business in Five Points in Atlanta selling poultry to walk-in customers but soon supplied processed poultry products to hotels and restaurants in the Atlanta community. As his business grew, he bought a company in north Georgia to raise chickens, and he built a feed mill and hatchery.

Jesse Jewell, from the Gainesville, Georgia History Museum. *Neely Young*.

Cagle followed Jewell's example by contracting with local farmers. Soon, they were supplying Cagle's hatchery with 2.6 million eggs. His company began selling chickens that were cut up and sold in individually frozen pieces that were breaded or marinated. The meals targeted working moms looking for easy-to-cook meals. They also supplied fast-food companies with frozen products, including ready-to-cook chicken nuggets that enabled restaurants to achieve uniform cooking results.

Cagle's small company formed in the 1940s and started with an $8,000 investment. Today, it is one of the top poultry producers globally, selling over 400 million pounds of chicken to food distributors, fast-food chains, restaurants and schools.

Sources

Georgia Poultry Federation. "Poultry Proud, Georgia Strong Since 1951." www. gapf.org.

Hutchens, Linda Rucker, and Ella J. Wilmont Smith. *Hall County, Georgia*. Black America Series. Charleston, SC: Arcadia Publishing, 2004.

Sawyer, Gordon. *Gainesville: 1900–2000*. Images of America. Charleston, SC: Arcadia Publishing, 1999.

BOBBY JONES

GREATEST GOLFER IN THE WORLD
MARCH 17, 1902–DECEMBER 18, 1971

Robert Tyre Jones was an amateur golfer often considered the greatest in golf history. He was born in Atlanta in 1902 and grew up playing golf at East Lake Country Club. He graduated from Georgia Tech, Harvard University and Emory University School of Law. He played in local tournaments during his college years but decided to pass on a career as a professional golfer and instead apply his energy to his law practice.

Jones had a bad temper and clashed with others. His early golf years were called his "Seven Lean Years," where he failed in any golf contest. But Jones soon learned to temper his emotions and became a gentleman on the golf course.

In 1930, Jones became famous for winning golf's Grand Slam—a feat achieved by winning the British Amateur Championship, British Open, U.S. Open and U.S. Amateur Championship in one year. No one else has been able to complete the Grand Slam in the history of golf.

He went on to win the U.S. Amateur five times, the U.S. Open four times, the British Open three times and the Walker Club five times. He led the U.S. Golf teams against the British amateur teams in nine of ten matches.

He retired in 1930 after eight years of dominating the sport. He returned to his law practice but did not stop his association with the game. He signed with A.G. Spalding & Brothers to design and endorse a line of golf clubs. He wrote several books on golf, including *Down the Fairway*, with journalist O.B. Keeler, and *Golf Is My Game*.

Bobby Jones. *Library of Congress.*

In 1934, Jones helped form the annual Masters Tournament at the Augusta National Golf Club in Augusta, Georgia. Many consider this his finest legacy. Wrote golf writer Herbert Warren Wind, "In the opinion of many people, of all the greatest athletes, Jones came to be what we call a great man."

Sources

Allen, Fredrick. *The Secret Formula: The Inside Story of How Coca-Cola Became the Best-Known Brand in the World.* New York: Open Road Integrated Media, 1994.

Jones, Robert Tyre "Bobby." *Bobby Jones on Golf.* New York: Doubleday, 1966.

Keeler, O.B. *The Bobby Jones Story.* N.p.: IQ Press Corp., 2003.

DR. MARTIN LUTHER KING JR.

I HAVE A DREAM
JANUARY 15, 1929–APRIL 4, 1968

Dr. Martin Luther King is considered the most influential nonviolent leader in Georgia—and U.S.—history. He oversaw the modern civil rights movement from its earliest days in the 1950s until his assassination on April 4, 1968, in Memphis, Tennessee.

Born in Atlanta, he was the son of Baptist minister Michael King Sr. and Alberta Williams King. His father served at Ebenezer Baptist Church, located in downtown Atlanta. King later followed in his father's footsteps by becoming a minister and social activist.

He grew up in a time of segregation, and his main goal in life was to end the legally separated status of Black and white Americans in the Deep South. He was inspired by the nonviolent methods used successfully by Mahatma Gandhi in India, such as civil disobedience and massive boycotts.

King started his religious life by serving as an assistant to his father at Ebenezer Baptist Church while attending Morehouse College in Atlanta. He eventually attended theological school in Pennsylvania and earned a PhD in systemic theology at Boston University. He became pastor of a church in Montgomery, Alabama, in 1954. As a member of the National Association for the Advancement of Colored People (NAACP), King led the first nonviolent demonstration in America, the Montgomery Bus Boycott, which challenged the separation of Black people riding city buses. The boycott had near-unanimous participation and lasted 381 days.

Dr. Martin Luther King Jr. *Library of Congress.*

King's home was bombed during the boycott. He was arrested, and his supporters were subjected to abuse. But the boycott and the crisis led the U.S. Supreme Court to declare laws requiring segregation on buses to be unconstitutional. After the ruling, Black and white people in the South could use buses as equals.

In future actions, King led massive protests in Birmingham, Alabama, where he was arrested and jailed. While incarcerated, he wrote his inspiring *Letter from a Birmingham Jail*, a manifesto of his philosophy and tactics. Later published, the letter caught the entire world's attention.

He directed a peaceful march on Washington, D.C., in 1963 and delivered his "I Have a Dream" address on the steps of the Lincoln Memorial to more than 250,000 people. In the speech, he called for economic and civil rights and an end to racism in the United States. He wanted white people to listen to the words and understand that Black and white people could live in a peaceful society together.

The text reads in part: "I say to you today, my friends, so even though we face the difficulties today and tomorrow, I still have a dream....I have a dream that my four little children will one day live in a nation where they will not be judged by the color of their skin but by the content of their character."

He met with President John F. Kennedy and other leaders of Congress to promote his cause. King's most significant political success was witnessing the creation of the Civil Rights Act of 1964 and the Voting Rights Act of 1965 by President Lyndon Johnson.

Throughout his eleven-year quest for equality, between 1957 and 1968, King traveled all over the South preaching to citizens to overcome laws that were causes of injustice against Black people. He was assaulted many times but became a world figure and was named Man of the Year by *Time* magazine in 1963. King received the Nobel Peace Prize in 1964, becoming the youngest recipient of the award at the time. He was only thirty-five.

He was assassinated in Memphis, shot by James Earl Ray on the balcony of his room at the Lorraine Motel. He was in the city to lead a march of striking garbage workers. A national historic site at his tomb and the Center for Nonviolent Change in Atlanta honors his legacy.

Sources

Carson, Clayborne, ed. *The Autobiography of Martin Luther King, Jr.* New York: Warner Books, 2001.

History. "I Have a Dream." www.history.com.

MILLS B. LANE

IT'S A WONDERFUL WORLD
JANUARY 29, 1912–MAY 7, 1989

Mills Lane was born in Savannah. After graduating from Yale University, he became the most famous banker in the South. He began his career as a clerk in his father's bank in Valdosta, rising quickly through the ranks to become president of the Citizens and Southern National Bank following his father's death in 1946. Lane made the bank one of the South's largest financial institutions and helped pioneer data processing and credit card services to customers. He was known as a leader of Atlanta's economic, political and racially progressive attitudes that propelled the city and the state during the economic boom of the 1940s, '50s and '60s.

Lane was a showman and a lovable character. He encouraged his bank to lend money liberally and created a carnival climate that was unusual for a bank. His directors would describe him as crazy, but crazy like a fox. He once paraded a flock of sheep into the bank lobby to promote the wool industry and another time came into his office wearing a football uniform to encourage teamwork.

He kept his office on the first floor of the bank so that friends and customers could walk in to say hello, and he wore a tie that said, "It's a Wonderful World." Soon all the company's banking executives wore the same necktie to greet customers.

In 1964, a major-league baseball team was looking to move to a new city and contacted the mayor of Atlanta, Ivan Allen, to see if Atlanta was

Mills B. Lane. *Courtesy of Special Collections & Archives, Georgia State University Library.*

interested. The city had no stadium to house a team, so Allen contacted Lane to ask for a loan to help. Lane agreed to extend the city a full line of credit to finance the construction of a stadium. The bank took a significant risk in assisting Allen because he was borrowing money to fund a professional sports facility with money it didn't have, on land it did not own, for a baseball team it had not yet signed.

After the stadium was finished, the Milwaukee Braves agreed to move their team to Atlanta. Called the "Miracle in Atlanta" in a book by Atlanta sportswriter Furman Bisher, the bank's risk paid off, making Atlanta the first southern city to have a major-league ball club. The Atlanta Falcons, Hawks basketball and other pro sports teams followed, along with an NHL franchise.

In 1971, during the difficult years of the civil rights movement, Lane and Black real estate agent W.L. Calloway formed the Action Forum to help defuse racial tensions. He also helped start the Commerce Club, which was made up of leading business executives working with Black leaders to achieve peaceful desegregation policies. Their efforts included adding Black members of the Atlanta police department, giving African Americans rights to sit with whites on public transportation and integrating Atlanta's public schools.

He helped form the "Committee of 100," an organization that promoted desegregation policies in his native city of Savannah. Citizen and Southern Bank branches were located in every major city in Georgia, and his leadership in those communities helped advance civil rights efforts.

In politics, he teamed up with progressive figures to help them get elected and to promote civil rights. He supported Carl Sanders in his successful campaign for governor against segregationist governor Marvin Griffin.

Lane retired from the bank and returned to Savannah, where he continued to be involved in civic causes until his death in 1989. He was called one of Georgia's great unsung heroes of his time. His positive expression, "It's a Wonderful World," was an inspiration to all.

Sources

Fowler, Glen. "Mills B. Lane, Jr., Atlanta Banker, Is Dead at 77." *New York Times*, May 10, 1989, section D, page 28.

Georgia Historical Society. georgiahistory.com.

Lester, Rex. "The Wonderful World of Mills B. Lane, Jr." Speech to the Beehive Foundation, September 12, 2016.

Mills B. Lane Jr. papers, 1852–1980. Identification MS 1914, Georgia Historical Society.

CONGRESSMAN JOHN R. LEWIS

TOWERING FIGURE OF THE CIVIL RIGHTS ERA
FEBRUARY 21, 1940–JULY 17, 2020

Born in Troy, Alabama, John Lewis attended public schools and later seminary in Nashville, Tennessee. While there, he became active in the civil rights movement and helped organize sit-ins at white businesses throughout Nashville.

His commitment to the movement grew. Lewis was among the thirteen original Freedom Riders, a group of protesters (Black and white, men and women) who opposed segregation in public transportation across the South beginning in May 1961. He and his fellow Freedom Riders were routinely harassed, beaten, arrested and jailed by white authorities.

Lewis became a leader in a new organization mobilizing students, the Student Nonviolent Coordinating Committee (SNCC). It was one of six organizations that helped plan the March on Washington, a massive civil rights demonstration. The six organization leaders—James Farmer, Martin Luther King Jr., John Lewis, A. Phillip Randolph, Roy Wilkins and Whitney Young—were known as the Big Six and became significant players in the future civil rights movement.

In what was called the March on Washington for Jobs and Freedom of 1963, some 250,000 people came together to demand equal pay and jobs for Black Americans. Standing in front of the Lincoln Memorial, Martin Luther King Jr. delivered his "I Have a Dream" speech. John Lewis was invited to be a part of the event and, at age twenty-three, was the youngest speaker at the demonstration. He called for all Americans to press for social and economic changes.

Congressman John R.
Lewis. *Matt Slocum/AP/
Shutterstock.*

On March 7, 1965, Lewis led a march from Selma to Montgomery, Alabama. While they were crossing the Edmund Pettus Bridge in Selma, police and state troopers beat and severely attacked Lewis's marchers. Lewis suffered a concussion and was hospitalized. The violent actions became known in history as Bloody Sunday.

Images of the Bloody Sunday march and attack were shown on television and published in newspapers throughout the United States and the world. Historians later credited the events of Bloody Sunday with spurring Congress to pass the Voting Rights Act of 1965.

Lewis moved to Atlanta and continued to fight for civil rights, entering politics by running for the Atlanta City Council. In 1986, he was elected to the U.S. House of Representatives representing District 5, Georgia's and Atlanta's largest district, with more than 700,000 people. He ran as a Democrat and was reelected sixteen times. Over the years, he opposed many of Washington's popular decisions, including the 1991 Gulf War, the 2000 U.S. trade agreement with China and President Bill Clinton's welfare reform.

He made an annual pilgrimage to Alabama to reenact his famous 1965 march from Selma to Montgomery; the route is included as part of the National Historic Trail system.

Lewis received many national awards, including the Profiles in Courage Award, the NAACP Medal and the Presidential Medal of Freedom. In 2016, a U.S. naval replenishment tanker was named USNS *John Lewis*. He wrote numerous books, including *March*, a three-volume graphic novel memoir.

Lewis died on July 17, 2020. He lived a life of sacrifice and service to all people, especially as an advocate for the poor, the disadvantaged and those who needed a helping hand and a voice to be part of the American dream.

Sources

Lewis, John, and Michael D'Orso. *Walking with the Wind*. New York: Simon and Schuster, 1998.

Seelye, Katharine Q. "John Lewis, Towering Figure of Civil Rights Era Dies at 80." *New York Times*, July 17, 2020. nytimes.com.

Woodward, Calvin. "Remembering John Lewis, Civil Rights and American Hero." AP July 18, 2020. apnews.com.

JIM LIENTZ

See entry for Mayor Malcolm Maclean (page 116).

GENERAL JAMES LONGSTREET
AND HELEN DORTCH LONGSTREET

A LOVE STORY OF CONFLICT AND REDEMPTION
JAMES: JANUARY 8, 1821–JANUARY 2, 1904
HELEN: APRIL 20, 1863–MAY 3, 1962

Few stories are more powerful than that of General James Longstreet, his feud with Jubal Early after the Civil War and the effort by his second wife, Helen Dortch Longstreet, to defend his name after he died in 1911.

In 1897, the seventy-six-year-old Longstreet married Helen Dortch, a woman forty years his junior. She was a newspaperwoman who wrote columns and became an editor and publisher of various newspapers. After his death, she became a fearless defender of his legacy and famous in her own right.

During the Civil War, Longstreet was Robert E. Lee's best general. After many losses, the victory at the Battle of Gettysburg in July 1863 was the turning point in the war for the Union. But the debate has raged for 150 years in the South about who was responsible for the loss.

During the battle, Robert E. Lee ordered Longstreet's division, led by General George Pickett, to charge Cemetery Hill. Lee felt that a Confederate victory at this position in enemy territory near Washington, D.C., could end the war. Longstreet disagreed and wanted to flank the Hill and have the advantage on higher ground.

Lee ordered Longstreet to take his division under Pickett's and charge the middle of the Union lines. But Pickett's charge was a disaster and resulted in a total Union victory. The victory turned the tide of the war, and the Confederacy never recovered.

General James and Helen Dortch Longstreet. *From James Longstreet Museum.*

After the war, a movement called the "Lost Cause" was formed, which advocated that secession, not slavery, was the cause of the war and that the Confederacy was defeated only because of the Union's advantage in more men and resources, among other beliefs. Many people south of the Mason-Dixon line believed the South's defeat was honorable and revered those who fought in the war. However, Longstreet thought that his native South should put the war behind it and accept Black Americans as equals. He did the unthinkable and joined the Republican Party, which at that time advocated for Black civil rights and supported Reconstruction efforts.

His good friend General Ulysses S. Grant appointed him to a position that was as powerful as governor of Louisiana. Southerners were shocked when Longstreet used Black troops to put down a white rebellion in New Orleans.

Former Confederate general Jubal Early was elected the head of the Association of the Army of Northern Virginia, a Confederate war veterans group. He wrote a long newspaper column blaming Longstreet for the loss at Gettysburg. For the next forty years, Longstreet became a Judas to many in the South.

Over one hundred years after the Battle of Gettysburg, the Pulitzer Prize–winning book *The Killer Angels* by Michael Shaara told the real story of the events and helped restore Longstreet's reputation. The movie *Gettysburg*, produced by Ted Turner, another famous Georgian, also helped set the record straight.

Longstreet retired to Gainesville, Georgia, where he married Helen Dortch and operated a large hotel. He died in 1904, but for the rest of her life, Dortch defended her husband's reputation and became famous for advocating for progressive causes and rights for women. She was known as the "Fighting Lady" and championed causes such as civil rights for African Americans and the environment. She was appointed as a delegate to the Progressive Party Convention and supported Theodore Roosevelt in 1912. Later, she was named the assistant librarian for the state of Georgia. During World War II, she worked with what is now Lockheed Aircraft, and in 1950, she ran (unsuccessfully) for governor against Herman Talmadge.

Helen Dortch Longstreet received many honors throughout the years. She became the first woman to have her portrait placed in the Georgia Capitol. She died in 1962 and was inducted as a Georgia Woman of Achievement in 2004.

Sources

Banks, John. "Longstreet's Second Lady." Historynet, April 2018. www.historynet.com.

DiNardo, R.L., and Albert A. Nofi. *James Longstreet: The Man, the Soldier, the Controversy*. Conshohocken, PA: Combined Publishing Co., 1998.

Georgia Women of Achievement. "Helen Dortch Longstreet, Activist, Conservationist, Postmistress." www.georgiawomen.org.

Longstreet Society. "Helen Dortch Longstreet." www.longstreetsociety.org.

Piston, William Garrett. *Lee's Tarnished Lieutenant: James Longstreet and His Place in Southern History*. Athens: University of Georgia Press, 1987.

Shaara, Michael. *The Killer Angels*. New York: Random House Inc., 1974.

JULIETTE GORDON LOW

THE BEST SCOUT OF THEM ALL
OCTOBER 31, 1860–JANUARY 17, 1927

Juliette Gordon Low was born in Savannah and founded the Girl Scouts of America. From her first troop in Savannah, the Girl Scouts now serve millions of young girls trained in the art of fostering their individual growth, character and self-sufficiency.

As a child, she experienced several ear injuries that left her with significant hearing issues affecting her for the remainder of her life. She was interested in sports, nature and arts. In 1886, she married William Mackie Low and settled in England. She was a force in English society and hosted many famous people, including the Duke of Windsor.

Her marriage to Low was rocky, and they separated when she found her husband had an affair with another woman. When her husband died in 1905, he left the bulk of the estate to his mistress, leaving Low with just a small annual allowance. She contested the will and won a large settlement, including all the properties in Georgia.

In 1911, she met Sir Robert Baden-Powell, the founder of the Boy Scouts. They became great friends, and he asked her to begin working with the Girl Guides, the Boy Scouts' sister organization in Great Britain. Through this work, Low was inspired to establish the Girl Scouts of America. She moved back to Savannah in 1912 and started the first Girl Scout chapter with eighteen girls. By 1925, there were more than ninety thousand Girl Scouts in the country.

Her many leadership talents included fundraising and public relations. As Girl Scouts gained more chapters throughout the country, she moved the

Scouts' headquarters to Washington, D.C. She made friends with the political figures of the day, including President Herbert Hoover's wife, Lou Henry Hoover. In 1917, Low convinced her to become the national vice president of the Girls Scouts. In the same year, President Woodrow Wilson's wife, Edith, became the honorary president of the National Girl Scouts. Low was famous and traveled back to England and met King George V and other notables.

Juliette Gordon Low. *AP/Shutterstock.*

During World War I, Low organized the Scouts to provide a program to help the troops by making surgical dressings and knitting clothing for soldiers. She started a thrift program to teach women how to conserve food, including growing and harvesting their own vegetables and canning goods. She established a camp in Cloudland, Georgia, designed to train girls and leaders together. Cloudland was named Camp Juliette Low.

In 1922, the annual Girl Scout convention was held in Savannah to celebrate Juliette Gordon Low and her accomplishments. She died in Savannah at age sixty-six. She was buried in her Scout uniform, with a note in her pocket stating, "You are not only the first Girl Scout but the best Girl Scout of them all." Today, the Girl Scouts of the USA is part of a worldwide family of 2.5 million girls and adults in ninety-two countries.

Sources

Cordery, Stacy A. *The Founder of the Girl Scouts, Juliette Gordon Low*. New York: Viking Press, 2012.

Girl Scouts. "Juliette Gordon Low, a Girl Scout." www.girlscouts.org.

REVEREND JOSEPH E. LOWERY

DEAN OF THE CIVIL RIGHTS MOVEMENT
OCTOBER 6, 1921–MARCH 27, 2020

Called the dean of the civil rights movement, Joseph Lowery was a part of the leadership that included Dr. Martin L. King Jr., Andrew Young, John Lewis and Ralph David Abernathy.

Lowery was born in Huntsville, Alabama. He attended high school and then went on to several colleges, including Paine College in Augusta, where he studied sociology. He received a call to preach and attended Payne Theological Seminary in Wilberforce, Ohio. In 1950, he was ordained as a Methodist minister and became pastor of the Warren Street Methodist Church in Mobile, Alabama. He soon became involved in the civil rights movement, fighting to end racial discrimination.

When Lowery was a college student in 1948, President Harry Truman signed an executive order declaring equal treatment and opportunity for everyone serving in the military. In 1954, the U.S. Supreme Court ruled that segregation of white and Black children in schools was unconstitutional. Lowery saw a way to apply these two rulings to change other laws discriminating against people of color in the South.

He helped lead the famous bus boycott in Montgomery, Alabama, after police arrested Rosa Parks, a Black woman, for refusing to give her bus seat to a white passenger. The bus boycott ended when the court ruled that segregation on public buses was unconstitutional.

He was a founder of and became the first vice president of the newly formed Southern Christian Leadership Conference (SCLC). Lowery was among the leaders of the Selma to Montgomery march. On March 7, 1965, some six hundred demonstrators tried to march across the Edmund Pettus

Reverend Joseph E. Lowery. *Susan Walsh/AP/Shutterstock.*

Bridge out of Selma when state and local lawmen violently attacked them with tear gas and rifle butts. Later that month, Lowery led a delegation to ask segregationist Governor George Wallace to support a march from Selma to Montgomery in support of voting rights. In response, Wallace directed state troopers to stop the march.

The March 7 confrontation, known as Bloody Sunday, and the Montgomery campaign ultimately pushed Congress into passing the Voting Rights Act of 1965. In 1995, former governor Wallace met with Lowery—along with two hundred others who had marched thirty years before—and apologized for what happened at Selma and for other actions during that time.

After several other church appointments, Lowery moved to Atlanta and became pastor of Cascade United Methodist Church. After Dr. Martin Luther King Jr.'s death, Lowery was named president of the SCLC, where he helped with marches and boycotts against racism in the South. In February 1982, he led more than 3,500 supporters in a march to Montgomery, Alabama, demanding an extension of the Voting Rights Act.

Joseph Lowery was a fire-and-brimstone preacher. In one sermon, he said, "I consider human relations to be a religious question. Human relations are based on our relations of God." In one of his most famous sermons, he preached, "The characteristics of the Kingdom are the goals of justice, peace, fellowship, and ending hunger and homelessness. I can't see leading people to make heaven their homes without homes on earth being heavenly."

In 2009, he gave the benediction at Barack Obama's presidential inauguration. He received numerous honors and awards, including the Lifetime Achievement Award from the NAACP. Clark Atlanta University also established the Lowery Institute for Justice and Human Rights; the City of Atlanta renamed Joseph E. Lowery Boulevard in his honor; and President Barack Obama awarded Lowery the Presidential Medal of Freedom at a White House ceremony.

Joseph Lowery died at age ninety-six at his home in Atlanta, fifty-two years after the death of his friend and confidant Martin Luther King Jr.

Sources

Lowery, Joseph E. *Singing: The Lord's Song in a Strange Land*. Nashville, TN: Abington Press, 2011.

Martin, Douglas. "Rev. Joseph E. Lowery, Civil Rights Leader and King Aid, Dies at 98." *New York Times*, April 9, 2020.

Martin Luther King Jr. National Historic Site. "The Rev. Joseph E. Lowery." www.nps.gov/features/malu/feat0002/wof/joseph_lowery.htm.

Suggs, Ernie. "Remembering Joseph Lowery: A Civil Rights Icon, 1921–2020." *Atlanta Journal-Constitution*, April 9, 2020.

SAVANNAH MAYOR MALCOLM MACLEAN,

BUSINESSMAN JIM LIENTZ,

GOVERNOR ERNEST VANDIVER,

ALBANY MOVEMENT PRESIDENT WILLIAM G. ANDERSON,

ALBANY COUNCILMAN THOMAS CHATMON,

COMMUNITY ACTIVIST FRANCES PAULEY,

ATLANTA POLICE CHIEF HERBERT JENKINS AND

FEDERAL JUDGE AUGUSTUS "GUS" BOOTLE

THE "BIG MULES": HOW WHITE AND BLACK LEADERS PEACEFULLY INTEGRATED GEORGIA SCHOOLS

While other southern state governors resisted the U.S. Supreme Court's 1954 order to integrate public schools (and eventually other facilities), leaders throughout the state of Georgia—Black and white, men and women—took a different approach.

Regretting his campaign pledge of "No not one," in speaking of integrating schools, Governor Ernest Vandiver realized he needed to come up with a way to peacefully desegregate Georgia's public schools in response to the *Brown v. Board of Education* decision. He appointed a state commission—the Sibley Commission, led by Atlanta banker John A. Sibley—which held hearings throughout the state to prepare cities and counties for the Supreme Court's ordered school desegregation. More than 1,800 Georgians appeared at the hearings. In the end, most agreed to move forward with integration

Georgia schools were the first in the South to be integrated. *Library of Congress, Prints and Photographs Division, LC-DIG-ppmsca-03089.*

and away from segregation, not only in schools but in other public buildings and businesses as well.

Later, when Black students Charlayne Hunter and Hamilton Holmes applied to the University of Georgia, Vandiver refused to defy the federal court's ruling, despite opposition from top state leaders. This move led to the peaceful desegregation of Atlanta schools several months later.

In other parts of the state, similar tactics were being employed. In Savannah, Black leaders called for a boycott of white merchants. The white mayor, Malcolm Maclean, met with the group to calm the situation. Mayor Maclean and white businessman Jim Lientz formed a "Committee of 100, made up of white business and community leaders. The committee stood with Black leaders and marched together into Savannah's segregated merchants and public facilities. With this biracial community support, Savannah became largely desegregated even before passage of the federal Civil Rights Act of 1964.

Meanwhile, in Albany, Black community leader William G. Anderson, white activist Frances Pauley and other Black leaders organized the Albany Movement to challenge the city's segregation policies. The group marched against the established white power structure in Albany, resulting in more

Library of Congress, Prints and Photographs Division, LC-DIG-ppmsca-03095.

than five hundred demonstrators jailed. Leaders of the Albany Movement asked Dr. Martin Luther King Jr. to come to the city to call attention to their struggle and secure greater national publicity for their cause. King was jailed several times while he was in Albany. In the end, he left the city believing the movement had failed.

But Black community leaders made decent inroads into Albany's political scene. Black businessman Thomas Chatmon ran for a city commission seat and forced a runoff election. King's efforts were successful when the city commission removed all the segregation statutes from its books in 1963.

In Atlanta, Mayor William Hartsfield appointed Herbert Jenkins to serve as the city's police chief during the civil rights struggle. Chief Jenkins took the opposite approach to Birmingham's notorious police chief Bull Connor, who attacked peaceful Black demonstrators with vicious dogs and fire hoses. In doing so, Jenkins brokered the relatively smooth and orderly integration of schools, libraries, shops, buses and restaurants in Atlanta. He hired the first Black officers in the police department and broke up an element of the Ku Klux Klan within the police department. He opened the state's first police academy, and his efforts won the respect of civil rights leaders, Black and white. When new mayor Ivan Allen was elected, he kept Chief Jenkins in charge and commended his strong stand for civil rights in the city.

Mayor Allen put together a coalition of Black and white leaders called the Big Mules. The group included Black businessman Herman Russell, Coca-Cola president Robert Woodruff, banker Mills Lane, lawyer Griffin Bell, businessman Richard Rich and many others in the business community who worked to desegregate the city.

Federal judge Augustus "Gus" Bootle was famous for his legal decisions desegregating Georgia public universities, public elementary and high schools and voter registration lists. When he first ruled in favor of Black citizens who were excluded from voter registration rolls, it opened the door to allow for class action suits by people of color to address integration issues. Before he passed away at age 102, he was asked, "Wasn't it hard to let Blacks into Georgia schools?" He answered, "It wasn't hard at all. Once you decide what's right, the making of it is easy. RIGHT is RIGHT!"

These tireless leaders, and those who went before them, helped turn other cities, including Augusta, Columbus and many other Georgia locations, into a beacon for other southern states, with progressive attitudes on race and race relations. Atlanta became the "City Too Busy to Hate," on its way to becoming an economic powerhouse with an increasingly diverse population.

Sources

Allen, Frederick. *Atlanta Rising: The Invention of an International City*. Atlanta: Longstreet Press, 1996.

Forwell, Lee. "The Albany Movement." New Georgia Encyclopedia. www. georgiaencyclopedia.org.

Jenkins, Herbert T., with James Sage Jenkins. *Keeping the Peace: Forty Years on the Force in Atlanta*. Atlanta: Darby Printing, n.d.

Jenkins, James Sage. *Atlanta in the Age of Pericles*. Lithonia, GA: Chimney Hill Press, 1995.

New York Times. "Savannah Is Tranquil." July 19, 1964, 1.

Young, Neely. "The History of Business Leadership Helped Sing the Song of Tolerance." *Georgia Historical Society Newsletter*, April 11, 2015.

LESTER MADDOX AND MARVIN GRIFFIN

RESISTANCE TO CHANGE:
CIVIL RIGHTS IN GEORGIA, 1952–1970
MADDOX: SEPTEMBER 30, 1915–JUNE 25, 2003
GRIFFIN: SEPTEMBER 4, 1907–JUNE 13, 1982

One of the most explosive actions in the twentieth century was *Brown v. the Board of Education*, the landmark 1954 Supreme Court decision overturning laws segregating schools and colleges. In 1896, the U.S. Supreme Court ruled that public facilities for Blacks and whites could be "separate but equal." Soon, southern states passed Jim Crow laws (so named after a derisive term for a Black man). These laws kept Black people separate but equal and kept them from gaining the civil rights afforded them by the U.S. Constitution.

Just two years later, the Supreme Court upheld a Mississippi law designed to deny Black people the right to vote. Soon, schools and colleges were segregated, and signs marked "White Only" and "Colored Only" were on public facilities, including water fountains and public bathrooms. In some states, Black people could not leave their homes after 10:00 p.m., and some cities passed Jim Crow laws that restricted Black people to living in certain parts of a town. Groups like the Ku Klux Klan and other hate groups used violence and lynching to punish Black men for even saying hello to a white woman. The *Brown v. the Board of Education* decision had the net effect of changing and canceling all of the South's Jim Crow laws.

Georgia governor Marvin Griffin declared he would protect segregated schools, "Come hell or high water." Griffin was from Bainbridge and grew up as a rabid segregationist. He was editor of his family's weekly newspaper, the *Post-Searchlight*, named for the community's location near the ending point of the Chattahoochee River in Lake Seminole, in South Georgia.

Lester Maddox. *Atlanta History Center*.

Griffin was not a bad governor; he was likable and told great, humorous stories. But he joined other segregation governors in the South to defy federal orders on desegregation. He changed the state flag to incorporate the Confederate Stars and Bars battle flag to resist, undermine and circumvent federal integration reform.

He declared, "There will be no mixing of the races in the public schools and college classes of Georgia anywhere, anytime as long as I am governor," in his State of the State address before the 1956 legislative session.

The state legislature passed other segregation laws, including "giving the Governor the right to close public schools and reestablish them as private segregated schools" and "giving the Georgia Attorney General the power to prosecute any action or threatened action that would violate segregation laws." Another law empowered the Georgia State Patrol to "make arrests and enforce any state law requiring segregation of the white and colored races." Federal courts later struck down all of these laws.

When Griffin ran for reelection in 1962, his campaign held large rallies serving barbecue to voters. But Georgia voters disagreed with his stand on blocking *Brown v. the Board of Education*. The state was ready for change, and Griffin lost to moderate Carl Sanders. Always ready with a quip, Griffin said, "Everybody that ate my barbecue, I don't believe voted for me!"

Governor Lester Maddox was another arch segregationist and restaurant owner whose outrageous defiance of the Supreme Court made national headlines.

Marvin Griffin. *Atlanta History Center*.

Maddox opened his Pickrick Restaurant in Atlanta in 1949 and started running racist advertising in the *Atlanta Journal* that promoted his political ideology. In April 1964, several Black college students entered his restaurant. Maddox ran them off his property using wooden axe handles he called "Pickrick drumsticks."

After President Lyndon Johnson signed the Civil Rights Act on July 2, 1964, three students tried to enter the restaurant, and Maddox escorted them off the property with a gun. Maddox gained national attention when he sued to overturn the law. When he lost the case in 1965, Maddox chose to close the Pickrick rather than serve Black customers.

In 1966, Maddox announced his plan to run for governor in the Democratic primary. He vowed to use the concept of "state's rights" to overcome the federal mandate to integrate public schools. He campaigned on the belief that integration was a Communist plot and that it was "ungodly, un-Christian and un-American."

In an upset, Maddox won against former governor Ellis Arnall, a political moderate. His opponent in the Republican election was Bo Callaway, but because Arnall's backers used a write-in vote, neither Maddox nor Callaway gained a majority. The Democratic-controlled legislature gave the election to Maddox. Atlanta native Dr. Martin Luther King Jr. said the election's outcome made him "ashamed to be a Georgian."

The legislature elected Maddox on the condition that he would agree to transfer the state budget process from the governor's control to the legislature. This change took power away from the governor from that time on, creating a ceremonial role for practical purposes.

Maddox kept his segregationist views but surprised his critics by initiating many progressive policies, including appointing many Black people to state government positions. He used his office to create an early release program for the state prison system. He was undoubtedly eccentric, and pictures of him riding his bicycle backward around the state capitol were featured in *Life* magazine.

After his term ended, Maddox was elected lieutenant governor and served for another four years. By that time, the state had changed and become one of the more progressive states in the South. Georgia's schools were integrated peaceably, and other changes were initiated to make Black people and other people of color welcome.

Maddox passed away at age eighty-seven, still maintaining his stand against segregation, believing he wanted his race preserved and saying that other races should want their race preserved as well.

Sources

Atlanta History Center. "Marvin Griffin." www.atlantahistory.com.

Bird, David. "Marvin Griffin, 74, Former Governor." *New York Times,* June 14, 1982.

Galphin, Bruce. *The Riddle of Lester Maddox.* Atlanta: Camelot Publishers, 1968.

Pomerantz, Gary M. *Where Peachtree Meets Sweet Auburn.* New York: Penguin Books, 1996.

BERNIE MARCUS AND ARTHUR BLANK

THEY REVOLUTIONIZED THE HARDWARE INDUSTRY
MARCUS: MAY 12, 1929–
BLANK: SEPTEMBER 27, 1942–

Arthur Blank and Bernie Marcus are co-founders of the Home Depot, the one-stop, do-it-yourself home improvement warehouse concept that revolutionized the hardware business. The Home Depot is the largest home improvement company in the United States.

Blank grew up in Flushing, New York, and graduated from Babson College in 1963. He was an accountant with Arthur Young Company before we went to work for his dad's small pharmaceutical company, which was bought by Darlin in 1968. Blank rose to become president of the company and later moved to another division of the company named the Handy Dan Improvement Company, where he met Bernard Marcus.

Bernard "Bernie" Marcus grew up in Newark, New Jersey. He attended Rutgers University, graduating with a pharmacy degree. He worked as a pharmacist for a cosmetics company and became interested in its retail side, where he moved up the ranks to be CEO of Handy Dan Improvement Company. In 1978, both executives were fired because of an internal power struggle between other officers in the company.

Both men had a dream to start a home improvement business retail center with a large warehouse concept. The two teamed up with investment banker Ken Langone, who assembled investors to fund the company. The Home Depot was founded in Atlanta in 1978 with just 2 stores. By 2020, it had more than 2,200 locations in the United States and its territories, Canada and Mexico. The company has more than 400,000 employees and generates more than $15 billion in operating income.

Bernie Marcus, *left*, and Arthur Blank. *John Bazemore/AP/Shutterstock.*

The Home Depot is the largest home improvement center in the United States, supplying tools, construction products and other services. Blank and Marcus became billionaires, and when they retired in the early 2000s, they invested their talents to improve Atlanta with significant gifts to community charitable causes.

Blank formed the Arthur M. Blank Family Foundation to promote positive change in people's lives and to enhance the communities in which they live. Since 1995, the Blank Family Foundation has granted more than $600 million to create social, economic and environmental value in metro Atlanta communities.

In February 2002, Blank purchased the Atlanta Falcons, the city's NFL team, from Taylor Smith. He also founded a Major League Soccer (MLS) franchise, Atlanta United Football Club, in 2014. The teams share Mercedes-Benz Stadium. The Falcons were NFC champions in 2016. They played the New England Patriots in Super Bowl LI in February 2017 and lost 34–28. In 2018, Atlanta United won the Major League Soccer U.S. Championship.

Blank has received several awards and honors, including being inducted into the Junior Achievement U.S. Business Hall of Fame and Georgia Trend Hall of Fame and being named Entrepreneur of the Year and two-time *Georgia Trend* magazine Most Respected CEO. He has been named a Georgia Trustee by the Georgia Historical Society.

Bernie Marcus became a donor of various charitable causes by funding the Marcus Institute, focused on providing services for children with developmental disabilities. Marcus also donated more than $50 million to Grady Hospital to build the Marcus Stroke and Neuroscience Center and the Marcus Trauma Center. Marcus was awarded the Others Award by the Salvation Award, its highest national honor.

In 2005, he contributed $250 million to launch the Georgia Aquarium, which opened in downtown Atlanta. According to the *Chronicle of Philanthropy* magazine, the Georgia Aquarium donation put Marcus and his wife, Billi, among the top charitable donors in the country. In 2009, Marcus was named a Georgia Trustee, an honor given by the Georgia Historical Society.

Sources

Blank, Arthur. *Good Company*. New York: HarperCollins, 2020.
Blank Family of Businesses. "Arthur Blank." blankfamilyofbusinesses.com.
Philanthropy Magazine. "Interview with Bernie Marcus, Prolific Philanthropist." www.philanthropyroundtable.com.
Rogers, Taylor Nicole. "Meet Bernie Marcus, the 90-Year-Old Billionaire Founder of Home Depot." *Business Insider*, July 23, 2019. businessinsider.com.

RALPH McGILL AND EUGENE "GENE" PATTERSON

JOURNALISTS WHO BECAME
THE CONSCIENCE OF THE SOUTH
McGILL: FEBRUARY 5, 1898–FEBRUARY 3, 1969
PATTERSON: OCTOBER 15, 1923–JANUARY 12, 2013

Ralph McGill and Gene Patterson were two significant figures in journalism during the civil rights era in the South. McGill was editor and publisher of the *Atlanta Constitution* in the 1950s and 1960s, and Patterson took over the role after McGill's death in 1969. Both won Pulitzer Prizes for their editorials describing the adverse effects of segregation in Georgia and the South.

McGill was a Tennessee native, originally a sports reporter and sports editor of the *Nashville Banner*. He moved to Atlanta in 1929 to cover sports, but he wanted to write more serious news and got his chance when he covered the Cuban revolution in 1933. By 1942, McGill was promoted to editor-in-chief of the *Constitution*. He was named publisher in 1960.

McGill used his front-page columns to highlight the problems of segregation. He became the only editor of a major southern newspaper to cover the passive resistance of Black groups, including those led by Dr. Martin Luther King Jr. His comments angered many readers of the newspaper, generating many letters to the editors. One night, someone burned crosses on his front lawn.

In 1954, when the Supreme Court struck down the separate but equal clause, McGill wrote about the dire conditions in Black schools versus those in white schools. He predicted that minority voters would someday have significant influence at the polls in Georgia and the nation. When his column was syndicated in the late 1950s and 1960s in hundreds of newspapers nationally, his voice became even more influential.

Ralph McGill. *AP/
Shutterstock.*

He visited Washington many times and became friends with Presidents John F. Kennedy and Lyndon B. Johnson. In 1959, he won the Pulitzer Prize for editorial writing, including his editorials on the Temple bombing by white supremacists in Atlanta in 1958 and hate crimes by the Ku Klux Klan. McGill died suddenly of a heart attack in 1969. He was inducted into the Georgia Writers Hall of Fame in 2004.

Eugene "Gene" Patterson was another prominent editor and publisher at the *Atlanta Constitution*. He also founded *Georgia Trend* magazine in 1985. He is best known for his columns written as editor of the *Atlanta Constitution* describing the dramatic social upheaval during the struggle for civil rights.

A native of Sparks, Patterson served as editor of the *Constitution* from 1960 to 1968. He wrote directly to his fellow white southerners every day, working to persuade them to change their ways. His words were so inspirational that Walter Cronkite asked him to read his most famous column, targeting the Birmingham church bombings, live during the CBS Evening News broadcast.

Here is an excerpt of that column, titled "A Flower for the Graves," written on September 16, 1963:

> *A Negro mother wept in the street Sunday morning in front of a Baptist Church in Birmingham. In her hand, she held a shoe, one shoe, from the foot of her dead child. We hold that shoe with her.*

> *Every one of us in the white South holds that small shoe in his hand.*
>
> *It is too late to blame the sick criminals who handled the dynamite. The FBI and the police can deal with that kind. The charge against them is simple. They killed four children.*
>
> *Only we can trace the truth, Southerner—you and I. We broke those children's bodies....*
>
> *...We know better. We created the day. We bear the judgment. May God have mercy on the poor South that has been so led. May what has happened hasten the day when the good South, which does live and has great being, will rise to this challenge of racial understanding and common humanity and is the full power of its unasserted courage, assert itself.*

Patterson won a Pulitzer Prize for the column in 1967. He resigned from the *Atlanta Constitution* in 1968 and became the editor at various newspapers, including the *Washington Post* and *St. Petersburg Times*. He taught one year at Duke University and later wrote a book, *The Changing South of Gene Patterson*. He died in 2013.

Other notable media leaders of this era include:

- Ray Moore, news director at WSB-TV and considered the Walter Cronkite of Georgia.
- Gravelly-voiced Aubrey Morris, along with Elmo Ellis, influential radio personalities for WSB radio. They stand in stark contrast to today's shock talk radio.
- Joe Cummings, who covered southern politics for *Newsweek*.
- Bill Emerson, southern correspondent for the *Washington Post*. Emerson later served as editor of the *Saturday Evening Post*.
- Tenney Griffin of the *Valdosta Daily Times*.

These journalists became the "Conscience of the South," leaving a legacy of courage for a changing South.

Sources

Clowse, Barbara Barksdale. *Ralph McGill: A Biography*. Macon, GA: Mercer University Press, 1998.

McFadden, Robert D. "Eugene C. Patterson, Editor and Civil Rights Crusader, Dies at 89." *New York Times*, January 13, 2013.

JOHN "JOHNNY" HERNDON MERCER

SAVANNAH'S AWARD-WINNING SONGWRITER
NOVEMBER 18, 1909–JUNE 25, 1976

Born in Savannah, John Herndon Mercer wrote more than one thousand songs, including winning four Academy Awards for the songs "Moon River," "Days of Wine and Roses," "On the Atchison, Topeka and the Santa Fe" and "In the Cool, Cool, Cool of the Evening."

He came from a fourth-generation Savannah family that included a grandfather who was a colonel in the Civil War. His father was a Savannah attorney who sent Mercer to high school in Virginia, where he continued his early interest in music. He especially loved Jazz Age music, including the songs of Louis Armstrong and other songwriters of his teenage years.

Mercer couldn't attend college because his father invested in real estate just before the 1929 Depression and had to declare bankruptcy. But his father's business troubles forced Mercer to head to New York and try his hand at being an actor. It quickly became evident that music was his strength. His first break came when he won a singing role with big-band leader Paul Whiteman.

Music culture was making the transition from sheet music to sound recording, movie musicals and radio, and Mercer thrived as a songwriter. He moved to Hollywood and became associated with major movie studios, including Warner Brothers, MGM and Twentieth Century Fox. He worked with Fred Astaire, Bing Crosby, Benny Goodman and Tommy Dorsey. When World II broke out in 1941, he wrote songs for movies, including popular tunes like "That Old Black Magic" and "My Shining Hour."

Johnny Mercer. *Library of Congress.*

In 1942, he co-founded Capitol Records and was challenging big record producers, including RCA Victor, Columbia and Decca. Nat King Cole and Peggy Lee were among the stars on his label, recordings songs like "One for My Baby (And One More for the Road)" and "G.I. Jive."

Capitol Records revolutionized the music industry, and Mercer made millions when he sold the company in 1955. One of the first checks from his company's sale was sent to the bank in Savannah to pay off his father's debts.

Mercer continued writing songs for movies like *Seven Brides for Seven Brothers*. He wrote the theme music for the film *Love in the Afternoon* and collaborated with Henry Mancini on one of his most famous songs, "Moon River," from the movie *Breakfast at Tiffany's*. Mercer even wrote the lyrics to a successful pop song, "Summer Wind," sung by Frank Sinatra.

He returned to Savannah and purchased a home on the Back River, the inspiration for his song "Moon River." Mercer died in 1976 and was buried in the family plot in Bonaventure Cemetery in Savannah. After his death, the City of Savannah named its municipal theater in his honor. He was posthumously inducted into the Georgia Music Hall of Fame (1980) and the Georgia Writers Hall of Fame (2011). The Georgia legislature declared April 19, 1995, Johnny Mercer Day in the state for "Mercer's outstanding contributions to the field of music."

Sources

Bach, Bob, Ginger Mercer and Johnny Mercer. *Our Huckleberry Friend: The Life, Times and Lyrics of Johnny Mercer*. New York: Lyle Stuart Inc., 1982.

Esker, Glen T. "Johnny Mercer." New Georgia Encyclopedia, August 12, 2003. www.georgiaencyclopedia.org.

Hutchison, Lydia. "Johnny Mercer." Performing Songwriter, November 18, 2017. www.performingsongwriter.com.

IMDb. "The Johnny Mercer Foundation." www.imdb.com.

ZELL MILLER

A POLITICAL FIGURE, BOLT OF LIGHTNING
FEBRUARY 24, 1932–MARCH 23, 2018

A dominant player in Georgia history, Miller served as a significant political figure in the last part of the twentieth century. He was nicknamed "Zig-Zag" Zell, which was fitting as his personality was described as a "bolt of lightning, darting this way and that and coming down with a crash!"

He served at nearly every level of elected office—including one year as mayor of Young Harris, Georgia; four years as a Georgia state senator; sixteen years as lieutenant governor; eight years as governor; and four years as U.S. senator. His total public service record spanned forty-six years.

Born in Young Harris, he was raised by his widowed mother and attended Young Harris College. He graduated from the two-year college with an associate degree in history and then enlisted in the U.S. Marine Corps for three years before enrolling at the University of Georgia in 1956. While there, he earned bachelor's and master's degrees in history and political science, married the former Shirley Bryan and then started his first job teaching history at Young Harris College. He wrote several books on politics and soon ran for mayor of the city of Young Harris, taking the first step that started his journey into the political landscape of the state.

Despite serving as chief of staff for Lester Maddox, Georgia's last segregationist governor, Miller moved past his history and went on to preserve the state's biracial coalition that gave Georgia its reputation as a progressive state. During his political life, he appointed African Americans to critical posts in the state government. Miller unsuccessfully tried to

Zell Miller. *Atlanta History Center.*

remove the Confederate battle flag from Georgia's state flag before Atlanta's Summer Olympics in 1996.

As governor, Miller became a national figure when he proposed the HOPE Scholarship (Helping Outstanding Pupils Educationally), a state-financed merit-based program funded by lottery ticket sales. Miller was concerned with the poor results of Georgia's lack of progress in its high school and colleges. The HOPE grants would pay four years of tuition and fees for colleges at Georgia public universities, college or technical institutions for students who graduated from a high school with a B average or higher. In 1991, Miller convinced the Georgia General Assembly to pass an amendment to the state constitution designating a statewide lottery to provide revenue for educational purposes only, and voters ratified the amendment the following year.

Miller stated that the educational program would have a three-fold purpose. He wanted to address the disparities between whites and African Americans and close the gap between college enrollment. He also wanted to improve the quality of education in high schools by incentivizing students to perform better with higher scores and encourage them to attend college.

Lastly, he felt the scholarship would encourage top-performing high school students to attend college in-state.

The HOPE Scholarship achieved tremendous results. Early on, 76.2 percent of first-time college students from Georgia received HOPE funds, including 97.1 percent of those students who attended the state's major institutions. In the years since, high school SAT scores have increased by forty points and freshman enrollment at state schools has increased by 15 percent. African American and other minority enrollment at all Georgia colleges has increased by 70 percent.

Many of the state's best students stayed in the state instead of attending other colleges out of state. The program benefited Georgia colleges and universities, as national ranking has increased dramatically since the advent of the program. More than $3 billion was awarded to more than 900,000 students by the end of the century,

Prior to Miller's election as governor, Georgia ranked low in educational outcomes for preschool children. His lottery proposal rolled out a pre-kindergarten (pre-K) program that would substantially improve early childhood educational outcomes. The pilot program started with 750 children from low-income families. The pre-K program was successful and expanded to serve more than 8,700 at-risk, four-year-old students. Later, it grew to accommodate more than 80,000 pre-K children statewide.

Studies of the state pre-K program showed that those who participated in the program had higher cognitive and academic results than those who did not. They had better results in language arts and math and fewer retentions. Miller's pre-K became a model for other states to follow and became the most extensive, most comprehensive preschool education system in the United States.

Miller also passed a "two strikes and you're out" law, enforcing lengthy mandatory prison sentences for those convicted of heinous crimes.

Polling showed that when he retired in 1999, Miller was the most popular Georgia governor in the twentieth century. But his political career was not over. Despite being his bitter rival, Miller's successor, Governor Roy Barnes, appointed him to the U.S. Senate. He was a Democrat, yet after he went to Washington, Miller became a supporter of Republican president George W. Bush. He wrote a book, *A National Party No More*, arguing that the Democratic Party had turned into a left-wing institution out of touch with America. Miller was a supporter of President Bill Clinton and spoke for him at the Democratic convention in 1992. But in 2004, he was a speaker at the Republican National Convention. Miller's combative speech received mixed reviews.

MSNBC anchor Chris Matthews interviewed Miller about his speech in which he said Democratic presidential nominee Senator John Kerry would leave the military armed with only "spitballs for defense." Miller told Matthews, "I wish we lived in the day when you could challenge a person to a duel!"

Miller stayed a stubbornly independent southern Democrat after he retired from the Senate. When his public career was over, he accepted teaching appointments to be a visiting professor at several colleges, including the University of Georgia and Emory University.

Later in life, Miller mellowed and made efforts at friendship with some of his political rivals, including political columnist Bill Shipp, with whom Miller carried a long feud over Shipp's negative coverage of his policies. At an event celebrating Shipp's eightieth birthday, Miller told the columnist that he loved him, much to the surprise of the audience.

Miller was an inspiration to the next generation of future twentieth-century leaders, including notables like Senators Johnny Isakson and Saxby Chambliss and Governor Nathan Deal.

In one of his books, Miller wrote, "I was born a Democrat. It is more a birthmark for me and for my fellow mountaineers. I would no more think of changing parties than I would think of changing my name." He died at Young Harris at age eighty-six at the home his mother built with rocks she used for the foundation.

Sources

Grant, Chris. "Zell Miller (1932–2018)." New Georgia Encyclopedia, October 7, 2005. www.georgiaencylopedia.org.

Hall, Aaron. "He Left a Legacy of Hope." *Georgia Impact Magazine*, August 23, 2018. news.uga.edu.

Miller, Zell. *A Deficit of Decency*. Macon, GA: Stroud and Hall Publishers, 2005.

———. *Zell Miller: A Senator Speaks Out on Patriotism, Values and Character*. N.p.: Monument Press, 2005.

MARGARET MITCHELL

GONE WITH THE WIND
NOVEMBER 8, 1900–AUGUST 18, 1949

Margaret Mitchell wrote *Gone with the Wind*, arguably the most famous book ever written by a Georgia author. She was a native Atlantan born into a prominent family and attended Smith College in Massachusetts after high school. She returned to Atlanta and married John Marsh in 1925.

She joined the *Atlanta Journal's Sunday Magazine* as a feature writer. She wrote on a wide range of topics, including a strange story about the clothes, uniforms and fashions of Confederate generals. Her stories about strong Georgia women created controversy among readers who believed the popular notion that women should stay at home and be housewives. Mitchell left the *Journal* after an ankle injury that would not heal properly.

Over the course of her three-year recuperation at home, she worked on a Civil War novel based on stories she heard as a child about the war and Reconstruction era. Much of the information came from her grandmother, who was a little girl during that time.

The novel was set in Georgia and depicted the struggles of Scarlett O'Hara, who lived on a wealthy plantation before the war, lived to see the property's destruction during General Sherman's March to the Sea and experienced struggles afterward. Mitchell was surprised that Macmillan Publishers in New York picked up her book, publishing it in 1936.

Gone with the Wind became a bestseller. It was popular with American readers and later became popular with readers worldwide. Mitchell won the Pulitzer Prize for fiction in 1937 for the book. It was adapted into a 1939

Margaret Mitchell. *Library of Congress.*

film that received the Academy Award for Best Picture in 1940. It is one of the most beloved movies of all time.

The book's popularity remained strong over the years. In 2014, a Harris poll found it was the second-favorite book of American readers, just behind the Bible. More than thirty million copies have been printed worldwide.

Modern journalists and other critics think the book and movie suggest that the enslaved people were depicted as happy and benefiting from their white owners. To many, it romanticized the Old South and the myth that the Civil War was not fought over slavery. But Mitchell was a feminist and believed her vision of Scarlett would encourage women and others to fight for equal rights for all.

Margaret Mitchell was killed by a speeding car driven by a drunk driver on August 16, 1949. She is buried in historic Oakland Cemetery near her parents. Her book continues to be read, studied in schools and beloved by readers around the world.

Sources

Allen, Patrick. *Margaret Mitchell, Reporter*. Athens, GA: Hill Street Press, 2000.

Atlanta Journal. "Margaret Mitchell Dies at 11:59 after Five-Day Battle for Life."
    August 16, 1949, section A, 1.

SPEAKER THOMAS "TOM" BAILEY MURPHY

CALLED MR. SPEAKER,
SERVED IN THE LEGISLATURE TWENTY-EIGHT YEARS
MARCH 10, 1924–DECEMBER 17, 2007

T om Murphy was Speaker of the Georgia House of Representatives for twenty-eight years, making him the longest-serving House Speaker of any U.S. state legislature in the nation. Described as volatile and witty with a personality as sharp as a ten-penny nail, Murphy served during five governors' terms.

He was born in Bremen, a city that was famous for clothing manufacturer Hubbard Pants. In 1943, he graduated from North Georgia College and enlisted in the navy during World War II. After the war, he attended the University of Georgia School of Law, graduating in 1949. He set up his law practice in his hometown, entered politics and was elected to the Georgia House of Representatives in 1961.

Murphy became influential in Georgia politics by the back door. In 1966, through a fluke, Georgia politics were controlled by the governor, who was a virtual dictator. The governor controlled the House and Senate committee assignments, what laws would be passed and what proposed laws would not be voted on.

Everything changed at the end of the 1966 governor's race when Democrat Lester Maddox and Republican Howard "Bo" Callaway ended their race in a tie, and neither candidate received a majority. Georgia law stated that if no one could claim victory, the race went to the legislature to decide. The Democratic-controlled House and Senate gave Maddox the governorship with the provision that the power to control the state

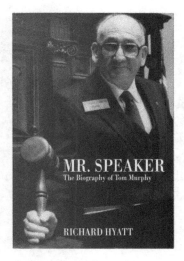

Thomas "Tom" Bailey Murphy.
Mercer University Press.

budget, selection of committee chairmen and other matters would move to the legislature. The change relegated Maddox and future governors to the position of figurehead, kissing babies and presiding over photo ops. Maddox had little power except to veto any legislation sent to him at the end of the session. When Tom Murphy became the Speaker of the House in 1973, he used a state constitutional provision that gave the House even more control over budget matters.

Murphy was viewed as a moderate in the new world of social change during the state's anti-segregation era. He was the architect of an alliance between rural white and urban Black Americans charged with running the state, even though he came across as a rude hick who stormed through the state capitol wearing cowboy boots and a large cowboy hat, chewing a big cigar.

He had a genuine concern for the underdog and said politics was designed to "give people power who have no power." He appointed African Americans and women to chairmanships of important committees and even brought them, including Republicans, into his inner power circle. He used his office to support children, veterans and people with disabilities.

He championed economic development in Atlanta and Georgia by financing public transportation, the Georgia World Congress Center and other state projects, including the Georgia Carpet Center in Dalton. He loved to visit with voters and would make time to see people who came off the street and asked to see him.

Murphy fought with governors, lieutenant governors and any Republican who dared cross his path. He was hard on Democratic House members, and he punished those who challenged his authority. Yet when he felt someone had learned his lesson, he would often bring them back into the fold.

Murphy's tenure as House Speaker ended in 2002 when he was defeated by Republican challenger Bill Heath. He suffered a stroke in 2004, and at his death in 2007, he was hailed by both parties as one of the most significant Speakers in Georgia's history.

Murphy was beloved by many in his hometown. After his death, the University of West Georgia re-created his cluttered office at the capitol as a part of its campus museum. He was a cigar-smoking country politician who took care of children and adults, both whites and Blacks, and made Georgia a better place.

Sources

Allen, Frederick. *Atlanta Rising*. Atlanta: Longstreet Press, 1996.

Atlanta Journal-Constitution. "Advocate for Atlanta: Tom Murphy: 1924–2007: Stalwart of the Statehouse." December 19, 2007. Legacy.com.

Goodman, Brenda. "Tom B. Murphy, a Longtime Power in Georgia, Dies at 83." *New York Times*, December 20, 2007. nytimes.com.

Hyatt, Richard. *Mr. Speaker: The Biography of Tom Murphy*. Macon, GA: Mercer University Press, 1999.

Murphy, Speaker Tom. Oral history interview, July 14, 1997. University of West Georgia, Special Collection. Available at Digital Library of Georgia. www.dlg. usg.edu.

FRANK HENRY NEELY

HE TOOK CHARGE OF THE FEDERAL RESERVE
JANUARY 19, 1884–MAY 24, 1979

Frank Neely was known for his administrative abilities in creating the "customer is always right" policies at Rich's Department Stores and as head of the Federal Reserve of Atlanta during the war years and later during the 1950s.

He was the son of Benjamin Neely of Rome, Georgia, the Rome School System's first superintendent. After his father's death, he moved to Cedartown, spending his teenage years there before graduating from Georgia Tech in 1904 with a mechanical engineering degree.

He married Rae Schlesinger and converted to her Jewish faith. He became a manager of the Fulton Bag and Cotton Mill, a large cotton manufacturing company with locations in Atlanta, New York, St. Louis and Minneapolis. In 1924, his friend Walter Rich offered him the job of general manager at Rich's Department Store. He became vice president, secretary, president and later chairman of the board of trustees. He was responsible for building Rich's into the largest department store in Georgia.

The company's influence was known throughout the South, especially for the lighting of a large Christmas tree and the Pink Pig ride that brought thousands of children to the store during the holidays. Neely's policy "the customer is always right" meant people could bring any purchased item back for a refund or exchange. Today, the practice is an industry standard.

In 1937, he was appointed to the Federal Reserve Bank of Atlanta and soon was named chairman of the board. While still serving as president

Frank Henry Neely. *Neely Young, from family collection.*

of Rich's, Neely ran the Reserve (as a volunteer), doing so with organization, operating efficiency, minimal waste and no duplication. He established a new research department and attracted a top-notch economist to turn the system into a powerful agency for conducting national monetary policy.

Neely was the longest-serving chairman of the Federal Reserve Bank of Atlanta (sixteen years). His stewardship spanned the Depression, World War II, the postwar rebuilding period and into the 1950s. As the southern regional director of the War Production Board during World War II, Neely was instrumental in bringing aircraft manufacturer Bell Aircraft Corp. (now Lockheed Martin) to Marietta.

Neely was the first chairman of the board of Georgia's Department of Commerce in 1948. He helped organize the Georgia Nuclear Advisory Commission, which helped bring a nuclear reactor to Georgia Tech. He received the school's Service Award and established a professorship in nuclear engineering. In 1963, Georgia Tech dedicated the Neely Nuclear Research Center in his honor.

He provided grants to Emory University, Georgia Tech and other institutions as president of the Rich's Foundation. He was honored as a true "Citizen of Atlanta." Neely lived a full life and died in 1979 at the age of ninety-six.

Sources

Gamble, Richard H. *History of the Federal Reserve Bank of Atlanta: Frank Neely Takes Charge.* Comp. by Franklin M. Garrett. N.p., 1989.

Neely, Frank H. *The Manager: A Human Engineer.* N.p.: self-published, 1965.

———. Papers, 1937–1969. Georgia Tech Library Archives, MS #088. library. gatech.edu/archives.

SENATOR SAM NUNN

THE BEST PRESIDENT THE NATION NEVER HAD
SEPTEMBER 8, 1938–

Senator Sam Nunn is sometimes called the best U.S. president the nation never had. His influence was strong during the thirty years he served in the Senate, notably for his efforts to stop the proliferation of nuclear weapons between the United States and Russia.

He was born in Macon and grew up in Perry, where his father, Samuel Augustus Nunn, practiced law and became mayor. Nunn was a star basketball player in high school and captain of the high school basketball team that won the state championship. He attended the Georgia Institute of Technology and Emory University, where he received his undergraduate degree and finished his law degree in 1962. After graduation, Nunn joined the U.S. Coast Guard and later served as a U.S. congressional staff member. He married Colleen O'Brien and moved back to Perry to join his father's law firm.

Nunn's political ambitions go back to his relationship with his great-uncle U.S. congressman Carl Vinson. In 1968, Nunn ran for the Georgia House of Representatives and won. At the end of his second term in the Georgia House, he decided to run for the former seat of U.S. senator Richard Russell, who had died the previous January. Russell's appointed successor was Atlanta attorney David Gambrell, who was considered a shoo-in in the next election. Nunn was unknown in Georgia's Democratic Party and an underdog running against the established statewide political machine. Most of his close friends thought he was crazy and gave him no chance to win.

During the election of 1972, Gambrell ran a traditional campaign using television and newspaper advertising and large political rallies. Nunn ran a nontraditional campaign, visiting every county in the state—speaking to small garden clubs, Rotary and Kiwanis Clubs and being interviewed by hometown newspapers. Nunn's campaign approach was to tell voters that he would be a moderate and make government work through cooperation and compromise.

Near the end of the campaign, Gambrell made a political error. During a debate, not only did he say he favored capital punishment, but he also said to those in the electric chair, "I will pull the switch." The comment came across as mean-hearted and cold. Headlines of "I'll Pull the Switch" ran in the national media, and Georgians were horrified as the campaign ended.

Senator Sam Nunn. *Shutterstock.*

Nunn won in a major upset in the Democratic primary that August, with 53.8 percent to 46.2 percent for Gambrell—a great victory. That November, he defeated Republican Norman Fletcher handily with 52 percent of the votes cast. Nunn was only thirty-three years of age.

Nunn made his mark in Congress early when he voted to extend the Voting Rights Act, giving fair and equal treatment for Black people and other people of color. Over the next thirty years, he honored his campaign pledge to work across the aisles with both Republican and Democratic members of Congress.

He was later named chairman of the powerful Senate Armed Services Committee. His legacy of accomplishment includes supporting President Jimmy Carter's Panama Canal Treaty, giving control of the canal to Panama. He joined with Barry Goldwater to pass the National Defense Act, which reorganized the Defense Department and did away with layers of bureaucracy, laying the foundation for better communication between the Armed Services.

When the Soviet Union broke apart in 1991, Nunn was concerned about what would happen to its large nuclear arsenal. He convinced Congress to pass the Cooperative Threat Reduction Act of 1991, which reduced nuclear warheads between the countries. Later, Congress passed the Nunn-Lugar-Domenici Domestic Preparedness Initiative, which prevented the use of weapons of mass destruction on American soil.

When Nunn retired from the Senate in 1997, he did not stop working on nuclear issues. He and Ted Turner formed the Nuclear Threat Initiative

(NTI), a private nonprofit organization that works to protect citizens around the world from nuclear, biological and chemical weapons.

Nunn's daughter Michelle continues in her father's legacy of public service. She is president and CEO of CARE USA, a nonprofit humanitarian aid agency based in Atlanta. In 2014, she ran unsuccessfully for the U.S. Senate.

Though he was often asked if he would run for president and named as a potential running mate for Barack Obama as he campaigned in the lead-up to the 2008 election, Nunn publicly declared his lack of interest in the post.

Sources

Brittanica. "Sam Nunn, United States Senator." Britannica.com.

Cockfield, Jamie H. *A Giant from Georgia, 1978–1957*. Macon, GA: Mercer University Press, 2019.

Georgia Tech. "Former United States Senator Sam Nunn." inta.gatech.edu/about/senator-sam-nunn.

McElroy, Roland. *The Best President the Nation Never Had*. Macon, GA: Mercer University Press, 2017.

FLANNERY O'CONNOR

WROTE ABOUT THE CLASSIC STRUGGLE
BETWEEN GOOD AND EVIL
MARCH 25, 1925–AUGUST 3, 1964

O'Connor was a short-story writer and novelist who wrote about life in the South. Her stories included a group of strange misfits and false prophets. She became famous when her first book, *Wise Blood*, became an international bestseller and was made into a movie.

When she was fifteen years old, O'Connor was deeply affected by the loss of her father to lupus. She graduated from Georgia College and State University in Milledgeville in 1945 and studied creative writing at the University of Iowa Writers Workshop. After college, she moved back to Milledgeville and lived a simple life writing short stories.

She published her first novel, *Wise Blood*, in 1952. It tells the tale of Hazel Motes, who loses his religion and starts a "Holy Church of Christ Without Christ" that is populated with an odd cast of itinerant loners and disenfranchised people. Motes's church becomes phantasmagorical, and he leads his membership into violent causes. The book concerns the relationship between God and the individual and Motes's search for redemption. At the end of the book, Motes blinds himself, saying, "If there's no bottom in your eyes, they hold more." He believes his eyes are so bottomless they can see the vision of God. When he dies, a pinpoint of light comes at the end. He is redeemed by the Christ he has tried so long to deny.

O'Connor's next publication, *A Good Man Is Hard to Find*, was her best-known work. The collection of short stories was published in 1955. The title story told the tale of an escaped convict named "The Misfit" who kills

Flannery O'Connor. *Everett/ Shutterstock.*

a family on vacation in the Deep South. The story's deranged character demonstrates startling acts of depraved brutality. The story's message illustrates the classic struggle between good and evil. For example, after The Misfit calls a grandmother a "good woman," he kills her, commenting, "She wouldn't stay at home and be queen for a day. Anyone seeing her dead on the highway would know she was a lady."

After the killings, The Misfit continues to believe he was a good man and thoughtful individual, as well as a cold-blooded killer. O'Connor uses the story's violence to form a divine stripping of The Misfit to return him to reality. By the end of the story, he can accept his moment of grace when he understands the difference between normal actions versus those that are not.

O'Connor developed lupus, the autoimmune disease that killed her father, in the 1950s. The condition, which had been in remission, returned in 1964, and she became gravely ill. She died at the age of thirty-nine and is buried in Milledgeville. Her posthumously published collection of stories, *The Complete Stories*, won the National Book Award for Fiction in 1972.

Sources

Biography. "Flannery O'Connor." biography.com.

Gordon, Sarah. "Flannery O'Connor (1925–1964)." New Georgia Encyclopedia, July 10, 2002. www.georgiaencyclopedia.org.

William, Joy. "Stranger Than Paradise." *New York Times*, February 26, 2009. nytimes.com.

EUGENE P. ODUM

FATHER OF MODERN FUNDAMENTALS OF ECOLOGY
SEPTEMBER 17, 1913–AUGUST 10, 2002

University of Georgia professor Eugene P. Odum was an internationally recognized pioneer in the study of ecology and the environment. His book titled *Fundamentals of Ecology* is the essential textbook for the study of ecosystems by students enrolled in universities all over the world.

He grew up in Chapel Hill, North Carolina, and Athens, Georgia, where his father was a sociology professor at the University of Georgia. Odum graduated from the University of North Carolina and received his PhD in ecology and ornithology from the University of Illinois in 1939.

Odum has been named the father of modern ecology—studying the relationship between living organisms, including humans, and their physical environment. Long before Rachel Carson's book *Silent Spring* changed the way people understood the world's environment, Odum was writing about how the study of ecology would help human mastery over nature.

For example, in the 1960s, ecologists determined that laundry detergents for cleaning and fertilizers used for crops contained large amounts of phosphorous (phosphates) and nitrogen that were dangerous to people's health. Armed with information about phosphates, federal and state officials, mayors and county officials were able to take action to require manufacturers to reduce these chemicals that harmed citizens. Many communities were able to restore streams and lakes, making them popular again for fishing and swimming.

Eugene Odum: Ecosystem Ecologist & Environmentalist, by Betty Jean Craige (University of Georgia Press, 2002).

Through ecological research, scientists found that many plants and animals produce chemicals that protect them from diseases. They used these chemicals to treat human diseases. For example, a substance found in horseshoe crabs located on the shores is used in leukemia treatments. Agricultural solutions include biological control of pests in crops damaged by insects and decreases in problems that are associated with harmful pesticides. Odum's early study of ecology helped propel much of this research.

In 1940, Odum accepted a teaching job at the University of Georgia, where he spent the next forty years. Under his leadership, the university became a world center for the study of ecology. He helped found the university's Institute of Ecology, of which he was named the longtime director.

Odum wrote his landmark textbook, *Fundamentals of Ecology*, with his younger brother, Howard, a graduate student at Yale. The book, which was published in 1953, coined the term the "habitat approach"; discussed freshwater, marine and terrestrial ecology; and included chapters on pollution, environmental health, radiation, remote sensing and microbial ecology. It was the only textbook concerning the subject for more than a decade and is still used as a text reference for students. *Fundamentals of Ecology* has been translated into more than a dozen languages.

In 1970, he was elected to membership in the National Academy of Sciences. He was later given the Tyler Ecology Award, an annual honor given for achievements in environmental science, by former president Jimmy Carter in 1977. Another citation was given to him when the Ecological Society of America named the Odum Award for Ecology in his honor. He began to appear in popular media like *Time* and *Newsweek* in his later life, as reporters asked him questions about environmental stewardship. Odum produced other books and attended and was the featured speaker at international conferences.

Before his death, the University of Georgia named the Odum School of Ecology in his honor. Eugene Odum died in Athens in 2002 at age eighty-eight. President Carter said of him, "Eugene Odum has had an important influence on the world by his insistence on the value of a quality environment. His pioneering work in ecology has changed the way we look at the natural world and our place in it."

Sources

Craige, Betty Jean. *Eugene Odum: Ecosystem Ecologist & Environmentalist*. Athens: University of Georgia Press, 2002.

Hataway, James. "Eugene Odum: The Father of Modern Ecology." UGA Today, January 9, 2018. news.uga.edu.

EUGENE "GENE" PATTERSON

See entry for Ralph McGill (page 127).

FRANCES PAULEY

See entry for Mayor Malcolm Maclean (page 116).

BILLY PAYNE

BROUGHT THE OLYMPIC GAMES TO ATLANTA
AND GAVE ATLANTA ITS FINEST HOUR
OCTOBER 13, 1947–

Billy Payne is the man who gave Atlanta its "finest hour," bringing the city the 1996 Summer Olympic Games. Born in Athens, Payne was a member of the University of Georgia football team that won ten games and a Cotton Bowl in 1966. He was a Phi Delta Theta fraternity member, belonged to the Gridiron Secret Society and graduated with a law degree in 1973.

Payne moved to Atlanta and started his law practice when he had the idea to convince former mayor Andrew Young that Atlanta could host the Olympic Games. He won support from Mayor Maynard Jackson and other community leaders to approach the International Olympic Committee to award the games to Atlanta.

The Olympics were usually awarded to international cities like Athens, London, Paris and Rome. Atlanta was a newcomer to the global stage. When Atlanta was selected in 1990, it was a big surprise to many.

The event was typically funded by national and local governments and considered money-losing propositions. Payne attempted to leave out most government funding and focused his efforts on financing the games from the private sector. With Young's help, a group called the Atlanta Nine navigated the politics, cost, planning and funding to make the project happen.

From 1990 forward, the city prepared for the games by building the Olympic Stadium, roads, venues and other infrastructure to host the millions of guests planning to attend the events.

The Olympic Games took place in Atlanta and other Georgia locations from July 19 through August 4. More than 2 million people came to Atlanta, and nearly 3.5 billion people worldwide watched on television.

At the opening ceremonies, eighty-three thousand people went to the Olympic Stadium and watched legendary boxer Muhammad Ali light the cauldron from the Olympic flame. The Atlanta Games included new Olympic events like beach volleyball, and new records were set in boxing, track and field, swimming and soccer.

Successfully hosting the games brought international attention to the city of Atlanta, and this was because Billy Payne believed Georgians would work together to make the event possible.

In 2006, Payne became chairman of the Augusta National Golf Club, home of the Masters Tournament. During his eleven years at the helm of the world's most famous golf club, Payne worked to bring more youth events

Billy Payne. *Jennifer Stalcup Photography.*

to compete after the Masters Tournament. He grew the club's reach and financial stature by expanding contracts with television coverage so viewers from all over the world could watch the Masters.

Before Payne became chairman, the club was an all-male membership. Payne managed to influence the direction of the club to welcome two female members. The board included former secretary of state Condoleezza Rice and business executive Darla Moore for membership to the Augusta National Golf Club in 2012. Payne received national recognition for the appointments.

In 2017, Billy Payne retired as chairman of the club. His other accomplishments include induction into the World Golf Hall of Fame, the National Football Foundation Distinguished American Award, twice being named the Georgian of the Year by *Georgia Trend* magazine and recognition as a Georgia Trustee by the Georgia Historical Society and Georgia governor's office, the highest honor the State of Georgia can bestow.

Sources

Allen, Frederick. *Atlanta Rising*. Atlanta: Longstreet Press, 1996.

Katz, Donald. "Billy Payne: Summer Olympics Boss, See Y'all in Atlanta." *Sports Illustrated,* January 8, 1996.

RICHARD "LITTLE RICHARD" PENNIMAN

HELPED START ROCK-AND-ROLL MUSIC
DECEMBER 5, 1932–MAY 9, 2020

Little Richard (Richard Wayne Penniman) was born in Macon, one of twelve children. Though his father was a bootlegger, Penniman grew up around uncles who were Baptist preachers and taught him to sing in church choirs. When he was a young teenager, he sang in church groups throughout Macon. He told the *Macon Telegraph* in 1987 that an entertainer named Esquerita taught him how to play piano. His first hit, "Tutti Frutti," was recorded in 1955 in New Orleans at J&M Studios. The record made him a star. The song was the first of many hits and helped him become a prominent rock-and-roll performer of the 1950s and 1960s. He performed on *The Ed Sullivan Show* on national television.

He was known for his showmanship and wild piano antics, pounding on the keys and dancing on the instrument's top simultaneously. His upbeat, screaming vocals were influential in creating and evolving several musical genres, including rock-and-roll, rhythm and blues, hip-hop, soul and funk. He inspired artists to keep pushing boundaries in those musical styles.

In 1956, his hit single, "Long Tall Sally," was number one on the Billboard Rhythm and Blues Best Seller chart. He went on to produce a three-year run of fifteen more hit songs, including "Good Golly Miss Molly," "Lucille" and "Rip It Up."

Little Richard elevated Black music that broke the color line, reaching audiences that were both white and Black. He influenced many other music greats, including Buddy Holly, the Everly Brothers, Jerry Lee Lewis, Eddie

Richard "Little
Richard" Penniman.
*Mark Humphrey/AP/
Shutterstock.*

Cochran and Bill Haley. Elvis Presley copied Little Richard's style, and
Presley performed several of Richard's songs on his breakthrough album in
1956. Presley told Penniman that his music was an inspiration to him and
that he was "the greatest."

In 1962, Penniman toured Europe and met a newly formed group, the
Beatles. They performed concerts together, and Richard capitalized on the
Beatles' popularity in England before they arrived in America. Richard
taught the group how to perform some of his songs and coached Paul
McCartney in developing his style of vocalizations.

Penniman was part of the first induction class of the Rock and Roll Hall
of Fame in 1986. He received the Lifetime Achievement Award from the
Rhythm and Blues Foundation and a Rhapsody and Rhythm award from
the National Museum of African American Music for his "key role in the
formation of popular music genres and helping to bring an end to the racial
divide on the music charts in the 1950s."

His first hit, "Tutti Frutti," is included in the National Recording Registry of the Library of Congress for "his unique vocalizing over the irresistible beat that announced a new era in music."

Little Richard lived a full life, dying at age eighty-seven of bone cancer at his home near Nashville, Tennessee. As one of the founders of rock-and-roll music, his flamboyant garb, wild piano music and shrieking voice embodied a new art form and the spirit of the age in the twentieth century.

Sources

Biography. "Little Richard: Death, Song & Facts." biography.com.

Rolling Stone. "Little Richard, the Pioneer Who Broke Musical Barriers." N.d. rollingstone.com.

White, Charles. *The Life and Times of Little Richard: The Authorized Biography*. London: Omnibus Press, 1984.

RABBI JACOB ROTHSCHILD

TEMPLE BOMBING SHOCK WAVE
AUGUST 4, 1911–DECEMBER 31, 1973

A native of Pittsburgh, Rabbi Jacob Rothschild was educated at Hebrew Union College in Cincinnati, Ohio. He was ordained in 1937 and entered the army as a chaplain during World War II. In 1946, he came to the Hebrew Benevolent Congregation, known as "the Temple" in Atlanta, and served as head of the synagogue for more than thirty years.

Raised in the North, Rothschild was surprised by the rampant segregation and racial policies in the South. Early in his tenure, he denounced segregation and the disenfranchisement of Black people. In one of his first sermons, he told the Jewish community in Atlanta that they should be active in opposing anti-Semitism. In the past, rabbis had avoided conflicts and worked with Christian church groups to keep peace in the city.

The South was a dangerous place for Jews and Blacks because of the region's bigotry and prejudice. Laws kept African Americans from voting in elections and out of certain public service professions. Regulations kept public schools segregated under "separate but equal," and the same laws kept Black students from attending public colleges and universities. Segregation extended to public restrooms and other facilities. With elements of the KKK still rampant in the South, Jews were also victims of the culture of prejudice, often banned from hotels, restaurants and clubs.

Rothschild's sermons continued to hammer on themes of racial justice. He invited members of the white Christian clergy to interfaith events held at the Temple and insisted on including Black Christian ministers.

Chaplain Fred W. Thissen, Catholic (*left*); Chaplain Ernest Pine, Protestant (*center*); and Chaplain Jacob Rothschild, Jewish (*right*), students at the U.S. Army chaplain school, Fort Benjamin Harrison, Indiana. *Library of Congress.*

In the fall of 1957, riots broke out as nine Black students attempted to enroll in Central High School in Little Rock, Arkansas. But while other southern cities were erupting in violence and threats of potential "blood in the streets" at the prospect of school integration, Rothchild saw his peacemaking efforts pay off as white Christian clergy embraced his words and Methodist Bishop Bevel Jones published a statement called the Ministers' Manifesto. It read, in part, "Freedom of Speech must at all costs be preserved....As Americans, and as Christians, we have an obligation to obey the law. The public school system must not be destroyed...and hatred and scorn for those of another race...can never be justified."

Atlanta mayor William Hartsfield agreed with the Manifesto, and influential members of Atlanta's white business community followed Hartsfield's endorsement. Hartsfield's leadership helped the city move forward on civil rights accomplishments such as integrating the police force, public transportation, the city school board, public golf courses and public high school.

Many Atlanta Temple leaders were fearful that Rothschild's aggressive policies would inflame pro-segregation whites. Their fears were realized when, on October 12, 1958, fifty sticks of dynamite exploded in front of the Temple entrance. The bomb created a massive hole in the front of the building, but no one was injured or killed. The Temple bombing sent a shock wave through the Atlanta community.

Rothschild soon received support from Christian churches, business owners and others who sent money to rebuild the facility. He heard from schoolchildren, veterans and widows, receiving more than five thousand letters and postcards.

Atlanta Constitution editor Ralph McGill penned a passionate front-page editorial. In it, he wrote, "For a long time now, it has been needful for all Americans to stand up and be counted on the side of law and due process of law, even when to do so goes against personal beliefs and emotions. It is late. But there is yet time." McGill won the Pulitzer Prize for editorial writing for his columns on the Temple bombing and other hate bombings.

Martin Luther King Jr. and Rothschild forged a personal relationship and friendship. Rothschild helped organize a city-sponsored dinner in King's honor when the civil rights leader received the Nobel Peace Prize and delivered the eulogy at a memorial service held by Atlanta's combined clergy following King's assassination. He continued to speak about social justice and civil rights until his death in 1973.

Sources

Blumberg, Janice Rothschild. *One Voice: Rabbi Jacob M. Rothschild and the Troubled South.* Macon, GA: Mercer University Press, 1985.

Greene, Melissa Fay. *The Temple Bombing.* Boston: Da Capo Press, 2006.

Rothschild, Jacob. "The Temple in Atlanta: The Temple Bombing." www.the-temple.org.

Stewart, Joshua. "Remembering the Temple Bombing and How It Changed Atlanta's Jewish Community." Georgia Public Broadcasting, March 25, 2014. gpb.org.

DEAN RUSK

ADVOCATE OF DIGNIFIED DIPLOMACY
FEBRUARY 9, 1909–DECEMBER 20, 1994

D ean Rusk served as secretary of state under President John F. Kennedy and President Lyndon Johnson during the Vietnam War.

He was born in Woodstock and attended Davidson College. He was a Rhodes Scholar and earned a master's degree from Oxford University in England. During World War II, he served under General Joseph W. Stilwell in the China-Burma-India theater and was later involved with the Korean War. Rusk was president of the Rockefeller Foundation in New York between 1952 and 1960 and worked to alleviate human suffering and promote democracy and philanthropy worldwide.

His experience working with Soviet Russia and the Far East (in both China and Korea) made him an expert in the two wars in that part of the world. He worked on Kennedy's presidential campaign in 1960, and after the election, Kennedy made him secretary of state. His role was that of an advisor who would preside over policy debates and endorse the president's decisions.

In 1961, Kennedy faced his first problem involving his new secretary of state. The Bay of Pigs fiasco occurred early in his administration when a brigade of American-trained Cuban exiles invaded Cuba and was defeated by Castro's Communist forces. In 1962, Soviet Russia snuck forty thousand troops into Cuba and installed nuclear missiles only eighty miles from Key West. Kennedy decided to order a naval blockade of Cuba.

To address the tense situation, he consulted with his presidential advisors to the White House, including his brother (U.S. attorney general) Robert Kennedy, National Security advisor McGeorge Bundy and Rusk. The U.S.

Dean Rusk. *Library of Congress.*

military was on its highest state of alert. For thirteen days, the government used secret back-door diplomacy between Attorney General Kennedy and Soviet ambassador Anatoly Dobrynin. At the end of the thirteen days, Soviet leader Nikita Khrushchev ordered the Soviet nuclear missiles' removal and sent Soviet troops out of Cuba. At the end of the crisis, Rusk famously said of what historians have named the Cuban Missile Crisis, "We're eyeball to eyeball, and I think the other fellow just blinked."

After President Kennedy was killed in Dallas, Texas, in 1963, Vice President Lyndon Johnson was sworn into office and asked Dean Rusk to stay on as his most influential advisor. Rusk's experience in South Asia led to his role in the Vietnam War. Rusk was a consistent proponent of U.S. participation in the Vietnam War and the "domino theory"—that without U.S. intervention, South Vietnam would fall into the hands of the Communist North. With Rusk's support, at its peak in 1968 there were 550,000 troops in Vietnam.

While the U.S. Air Force began bombing North Vietnam, Johnson's critics called for a peace initiative. Rusk rejected all these efforts and stated that the war was a test of Asia's ability to withstand the threat of one billion Chinese, armed with nuclear weapons. Rusk explained to the nation that if America stopped the North Vietnamese now, it would not have to wage a larger war later. Rusk was reviled by antiwar protesters who mobbed his public appearances shouting insults and "Stop the bombing!"

Eventually, President Richard Nixon withdrew U.S. forces, North Vietnam took over South Vietnam and more than fifty thousand American troops were killed. Critics of the withdrawal said, "It was the only war that America lost."

Rusk advocated what he called "dignified diplomacy" that emphasized communication and respect between the Soviet Union and the United States. His policy worked and helped the successful negotiation of the Limited Nuclear Test Ban Treaty in 1963.

He retired after leaving office in 1969. Rusk accepted a professorship teaching international law at the University of Georgia, which later established the Dean Rusk International Law Center. His memoir titled *As I Saw It* was published in 1990. He was a popular figure on campus during his later life. Dean Rusk Middle School in Cherokee County was named in his honor. Rusk passed away in Athens on December 20, 1994.

Sources

French, Jana. "Former Professor Advised JFK before Bringing Wisdom to UGA." The Red and Black, January 30, 2014. redandblack.com.

Rockefeller Foundation. "Dean Rusk." rockfound.rockarch.org.

Rusk, Dean. *The Winds of Freedom.* Boston: Beacon Press, 1963.

Rusk, Dean, and Tom Rusk. *As I Saw It.* New York: W.W. Norton & Company, 1990.

University of Georgia, School of Law. "Remembering Dean Rusk." law.uga.edu.

HERMAN RUSSELL

HE BROKE THROUGH SEGREGATION
AND BUILT AN EMPIRE
DECEMBER 23, 1930–NOVEMBER 15, 2014

Herman Russell created one of the nation's largest minority-owned real estate, construction and concessions empires. The H.J. Russell Company has $200 million in annual revenue, with more than 2,500 employees nationwide. Russell was a key figure during the 1960s civil rights movement as he provided support for leaders like Dr. Martin Luther King Jr. and others.

Russell grew up in the Jim Crow South, when the opportunities for Black people were limited. At age twelve, he decided to open a shoeshine business near his home in Atlanta's Summerhill neighborhood. Russell sold Coca-Cola, candy and other items and was so successful that at age sixteen, he purchased a partial piece of land near his home. He and his friends built a duplex on the vacant lot, and with the rental income he saved up, he was able to pay for his college education at Tuskegee Institute.

After graduation, he formed his real estate company, and by the 1960s, he was building residential developments and large apartment projects. Russell possessed excellent business and political judgment and used his skill to break into a profession and city dominated by white real estate developers. He became the first Black member of the Metro Atlanta Chamber of Commerce and was later named president of the organization.

As the city opened to minority developers, his company participated in many new projects, including the expansion of Hartsfield-Jackson Atlanta International Airport, sports facilities such as the Georgia Dome and the State Farm Arena across from Centennial Olympic Park.

Herman Russell.
Atlanta History Center.

The white political community liked Russell, and he leveraged that into support for Black political candidates for mayor—Maynard Jackson and Andrew Young.

His success went beyond Atlanta, as the company opened airport restaurant concessions across the country and overseas. In 1997, *Black Enterprise* magazine ranked Russell's company as the eighth-largest Black-owned enterprise in the United States.

Russell was a friend of presidents, congressmen, mayors and those who admired him for being a leader of people. He was a prominent philanthropist and gave $4 million to three Black colleges to establish entrepreneurship programs for young adults. He received multiple awards, including the 1991 Horatio Alger Award; was selected a Georgia Trustee by the Georgia Historical Society; was named to the International Civil Rights Walk of Fame; and was named to *Georgia Trend* magazine's Hall of Fame.

Ironically, when Atlanta was named the site of the 1996 Centennial Olympic Games, the decision was made to build the Olympic stadium in the Summerhill neighborhood in southeast Atlanta, the same area in which Herman Russell had grown up. His firm helped build the Olympic stadium. Russell's autobiography, *Building Atlanta*, was published in 2014, shortly before his death at age eighty-three. His children—two sons and one daughter—now run the company.

Sources

McKinney, Jeffrey. "Building Atlanta: The Story of Herman Russell." *Black Enterprise*, February 12, 2020. blackenterprise.com.

Poole, Shelia M. "Herman J. Russell Built an Empire." *Atlanta Journal-Constitution*, February 14, 2020.

Russell, Herman J., and Bob Andelman. *Building Atlanta: How I Broke Through Segregation to Launch a Business Empire*. Chicago: Chicago Review Press, 2014.

SENATOR RICHARD B. RUSSELL

A SENATOR'S SENATOR
NOVEMBER 2, 1897–JANUARY 21, 1971

Richard Russell was a native of Winder. His father was chief justice of Georgia's Supreme Court, and his mother was an educator who was named Georgia Mother of the Year. He graduated from the University of Georgia School of Law and started practicing law in his hometown. He ran as a Democrat for the Georgia House of Representatives, where he served as Speaker of House and was later elected governor of Georgia. After his term ended, Russell ran for and won a seat in the U.S. Senate in 1932.

At age twenty-three, Russell was one of the youngest U.S. senators at the time of his election. He served in Congress for over forty years. He was an authority on Senate rules and procedures. Strong on defense, Russell chaired the prestigious Armed Services Committee during two wars, including the Korean War. Russell also served on the Warren Commission, a special presidential commission related to the assassination of President Kennedy.

In 1946, he authored the National School Lunch Act, which provides meals to low-income students, and he created a subsidy system for farmers. He promoted new forms of energy, including the Vogtle Power Nuclear Plant in Augusta. He helped establish the Centers for Disease Control and Prevention (CDC) located in Atlanta, and he helped bring many other federal programs to Georgia. Russell Lake and Dam in Elberton and the Richard Russell Research Center in Athens are named in his honor.

In 1956, he co-authored the "Southern Manifesto" to oppose racial equality and led some Senate leaders to vote against the Civil Rights Act of 1964. His support for the states' rights movement hampered his ability to be elected president. Yet he earned such respect from his fellow senators that they named the Russell Senate Office Building in Washington in his honor.

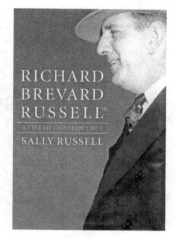

Senator Richard B. Russell.
Mercer University Press.

When he died, his body lay in the Georgia Capitol rotunda before he was buried near his home in Winder. President Richard Nixon called him a giant and said, "He possessed an unprecedented abundance, a rare blend of courage, character, vision, and ability that moved him indisputably into the ranks of those giants who have served in the United States Senate."

A Georgia historical marker is near his childhood home in Winder. The Richard B. Russell Jr. Special Collection Libraries and its Richard B. Russell Jr. Library for Political Research and Studies at the University of Georgia are named in his honor.

Sources

Russell, Richard. Papers, collection number RBRL/001/RBR. russelldoc.galib. uga.edu.

Russell, Sally. *Richard Brevard Russell Jr.: A Life of Consequence*. Macon, GA: Mercer University Press, 2011.

United States Senate. "Richard Russell: A Featured Biography." senate.gov.

GOVERNOR CARL EDWARD SANDERS SR.

REVERSED ANTI-BLACK POLICIES IN GEORGIA
MAY 15, 1925–NOVEMBER 16, 2014

C arl Sanders Sr. was born in Augusta and attended the University of Georgia. He was an outstanding student and elected to many college organizations, including Chi Phi, the Gridiron Secret Society and the Phi Kappa Literary Society.

During World War II, Sanders enlisted in the army and became a B-17 bomber pilot. After the war, he returned to school and earned his law degree.

He returned to Augusta, started his law practice and began his political career in 1954. He was elected to Georgia's House of Representatives and later to the state senate. Sanders was elected governor in 1962 at the age of thirty-seven. At the time, he was the youngest governor in the nation.

Reversing other southern states' anti-Black policies, Sanders denounced racially segregated schools and enforced federal laws on many civil rights issues, including giving voting rights to Black Americans. He refused to join other southern states fighting to keep the schools separate, and he removed "Whites Only" signs from the state capitol and other offices.

He supported John F. Kennedy's run for president and became one of President Lyndon Johnson's chief supporters after Kennedy's death. Sanders named two Black officers as Georgia delegates to the Democratic National Convention, stating, "This is a political organization, and it is right that we have a cross-section of the voters of the state represented." White voters opposed the appointments. This decision would come back to hurt Sanders in future campaigns.

Because he increased state funding for schools and developed community colleges around the state, he was called the "Education Governor." Sanders also played a part in bringing professional sports clubs to Atlanta, including the National Football League's Atlanta Falcons and Major League Baseball's Atlanta Braves.

Governor Carl Edward Sanders Sr. *Mercer University Press.*

Sanders's progressive stand on race and segregation promoted Georgia as a region that welcomed diversity and as a place of calm during the conflict in other states in the South. In 1960, both Atlanta and Birmingham, Alabama, had the same population, around 1 million people. But today, in part because of Georgia's evolving attitudes concerning race, the metro Atlanta population stands at 6 million, while Birmingham's has not grown substantially since that time, with a population of 1.2 million.

Sanders ran for governor again in 1970 but was defeated by Jimmy Carter. Carter and Sanders ran a bitter campaign where Carter portrayed Sanders as being too sympathetic to Black people.

After the election, Sanders retired from public service and founded Troutman Sanders law firm (now Troutman Pepper), one of the state's top law firms. He died at age eighty-nine and is remembered as a man who set the stage for Georgia's liberal reputation on race relations. President Jimmy Carter said that "Sanders was an outstanding governor of Georgia, a champion of education and a courageous proponent of ending racial segregation in our state."

Sources

Clowse, Barbara Barksdale. *Ralph McGill: A Biography*. Macon, GA: Mercer University Press, 1998.

Cook, James F. *Carl Sanders: Spokesman of the New South*. Macon, GA: Mercer University Press, 1993.

DOUG SANDERS

GOLFING GREAT WHO MISSED A THREE-FOOT PUTT
TO LOSE THE BRITISH OPEN
JULY 24, 1933–APRIL 12, 2020

G olfing great Doug Sanders won twenty PGA championships between 1956 and 1972. He grew up poor and was a sharecropper's son, born on a farm in Cedartown. As a boy, he picked cotton for ten cents a bag and collected golf balls at a country club near his home. Sanders learned to play golf there and was noted for an unusually short backswing that would drive the ball farther than anyone on the course. Several members at the club noticed that he had a gift for the sport. When he graduated from high school, they encouraged him to apply for a golf scholarship at Florida State University.

While in college, Sanders became a top golfer and developed a habit of wearing brightly colored clothes. His friends nicknamed him the "Peacock of the Fairways." His first victory was at the Canadian Open, the first amateur ever to win the tournament.

Sanders turned pro in 1957 and won his first victory at the Western Open. He came in second at the 1959 PGA Championship. During the 1960s, he placed in the top ten in all the major tournaments and won three other championships. The "Peacock of the Fairways" was a favorite with fans. He loved to talk with his audiences, telling them jokes and showing them trick shots during practice rounds. He was most famous for a missed putt.

Sanders was in first place at the last hole of the 1970 British Open played at the Old Course at St. Andrews in Scotland. He was on the edge of the green with a three-foot putt to the hole. All he had to do was make this small putt to win the tournament. To the horror of his fans, Sanders missed the

Frank Sinatra and Doug Sanders smile at Bermuda Dunes in California during the fourth round of the Bob Hope Desert Golf Classic, February 10, 1973. *AP/Shutterstock.*

putt and then lost the Open to Jack Nicklaus in a playoff. The event haunted him all his life; he still talked about the putt years later.

Sanders retired from golf and moved to Houston, Texas, where he created the Doug Sanders Celebrity Classic Tournament. He ran the event for several years and became friends with celebrities, presidents and astronauts. He is a member of the World Golf Hall of Fame, Georgia Golf Hall of Fame, Georgia Sports Hall of Fame, Florida Sports Hall of Fame and University of Florida Athletic Hall of Fame.

After his death at age eighty-six, his hometown of Cedartown opened the Doug Sanders Golf Museum to display his extensive collection of golf memorabilia obtained through his career as a professional golfer. Before his death, still remembering the loss of the putt at the British Open, he said, "My agent told me that putt cost me millions. But I can't complain. I've been blessed to have the career I had."

Sources

Goldstein, Richard. "Doug Sanders, Peacock of the Fairways, Dies at 86." *New York Times*, April 12, 2020. www.nytimes.com.

Stewart, Jeremy. "Doug Sanders Golf Museum Opens in Cedartown." *Polk County Standard Journal*, August 29, 2020. www.Polkstandardjournal.com.

ROBERT "BOB" SCHERER

HE KEPT THE LIGHTS ON IN GEORGIA
NOVEMBER 29, 1925–JANUARY 26, 2008

B ob Scherer was president of Georgia Power Company. In the 1970s, Georgia Power was practically bankrupt when Scherer became president. His swift actions turned the company around when the lights nearly went out in Georgia.

Born in St. Louis, Missouri, Bob Scherer graduated from Emory University Law School in 1946. He married and joined Georgia Power as a draftsman. Over the years, he moved up the corporate ladder, finally becoming president of the company. Georgia Power serves almost all of the state's 159 counties and provides electricity to more than 2.5 million residential customers.

Scherer's leadership was put to the test in 1975 when he became the company's president and discovered it was in dire financial shape. Simultaneously, the 1973 OPEC Oil Embargo drove up fuel prices, causing double-digit inflation and interest rates to soar.

The country was in a deep recession, and Georgia Power had several expensive power plants under construction. At the same time, it needed regular operating funds to keep the company running. Scherer went to New York to approach several large banks for a loan to get the company over the crisis. He was surprised when the banks turned him down.

Scherer was known to have a great personality. When he returned to Atlanta, he told his staff, "I was sort of like the fellow who threw a party, and nobody came."

Summoning the company's senior management, Scherer held meetings over several days to develop a strategy that would get the company out of the crisis. He took an optimistic approach and delivered a message

Robert Scherer. *Georgia Power.*

of hope—to the employees first and then the public. The company took out a series of newspaper ads informing readers that Georgia Power was committed to remaining open and communicating with its customers. The approach worked. By the end of the year, the company had become a more robust operation.

Scherer worked with the Georgia Public Service Commission and other government agencies to grant the company a rate increase. He negotiated a partnership with Georgia's Electric Membership Cooperatives (EMC), a nonprofit powered supply company, and Georgia's city Municipal Electric Authority to buy into Georgia Power generation plants. In what was called Scherer's "big bet," he saved the company and restored its stability for the future.

In 1985, Scherer partnered with the Salvation Army to assist people dealing with emergencies and challenging economic situations who needed food, clothing, shelter and help to pay their utility bills. The program was called Project SHARE and proved an easy way for people to help others in need. Customers could add $1, $2 or $10 to their monthly utility bill payment, and Georgia Power would match the monthly donation. The successful program assists more than fifty thousand Georgians annually. Over the years, Project SHARE has collected $72 million to give to those in need, a number that would fill a whole stadium full of people.

Scherer retired as chairman in 1989, having served as an active Georgia Power employee for forty-three years. At the time of his death in 2008, Georgia Power was the largest utility in the Southeast. The company named one of its electric plants in Monroe County the Robert W. Scherer Power Plant to honor him. He is remembered as the man "who, during a hard time, kept the lights on in Georgia."

Sources

Powell, Kay. "Bob Scherer, 82, He Took Charge at Georgia Power." www.legacy.com.
Taft, Dub, and Sam Heys. "Big Bets, Decisions and Leaders That Shaped Southern Company." Southern Company, 2011.

BILL SHIPP

OUTSPOKEN AND DISTINGUISHED
POLITICAL JOURNALIST
AUGUST 16, 1933-

B orn in Marietta, Bill Shipp is one of Georgia's most distinguished political journalists. His career spans more than fifty years as a writer for the *Atlanta Constitution* and *Georgia Trend* magazine, and he founded *Bill Shipp's Georgia*, a statewide weekly newsletter.

In 1955, when he was a college student, Shipp became famous when he wrote columns for the University of Georgia student newspaper, the *Red and Black*. Shipp wrote editorials criticizing the university president, the Georgia legislature and, most importantly, Georgia governor Herman Talmadge over their decision to deny Horace Ward, a Black man, admittance to UGA's law school. One editorial in the *Red and Black* called Talmadge "an unfit Governor."

Shipp's stories were picked up by state newspapers and other media outlets of the day and caused major distress for the state's political figures. University administrators and faculty made it clear to Shipp that they would all be more comfortable if he left, so Shipp quit school and joined the army. Later, Horace Ward became the first African American to serve as a United States Superior Court judge on the Southern District.

After returning from the Korean War, Shipp joined the *Atlanta Constitution* and became the premier investigative and political columnist in Georgia for the next thirty years. He wrote an award-winning series exposing racketeering and corruption in the Atlanta police force. He covered the civil rights movement and other significant stories, including breaking the early news that Jimmy Carter was running for president of the United States.

In the early years of the internet, he resigned from his job at the newspaper and started a printed and online newspaper called *Bill Shipp's Georgia*. The publication became a hit with readers all over the state. With his in-depth knowledge and command of the issues, he was a regular panelist on *The Georgia Gang*, a weekly public affairs television show, and a frequent moderator of political debates. Shipp also wrote twice-weekly columns that appeared in statewide daily and weekly newspapers and was named political editor for *Georgia Trend* magazine, a business, economic development and political magazine with fifty thousand subscribers across Georgia.

Bill Shipp. *Mercer University Press.*

Shipp authored several books, including *The Ape-Slayer and Other Snapshots*, a collection of his columns, and *Murder at Broad River Bridge: The Slaying of Lemuel Penn by Members of the Ku Klux Klan*, which was widely read and reprinted several times by the University of Georgia Press. His writing style was blunt and pulled no punches. For example, Shipp's book stated that the reason Penn was murdered was that he was a Black man on his way to see his wife in another state.

He received many awards from organizations such as the Associated Press, the Georgia Press Association and the Atlanta Press Club. In 1988, he received the Whittier Award for Lifetime Achievement in Journalism, and in 2016, Shipp was inducted into the Georgia Writers Hall Fame.

Sources

Shipp, Bill. *The Ape-Slayer and Other Snapshots*. Macon, GA: Mercer University Press, 1997.

———. *Murder at Broad River Bridge: The Slaying of Lemuel Penn by the Ku Klux Klan*. Athens: University of Georgia Press, 1981.

JOHN SIBLEY

A HERO OF ALL RACES
JANUARY 4, 1888–OCTOBER 26, 1986

Sibley was a lawyer and key figure in the integration of Georgia's schools. Born in 1888 near Milledgeville, Sibley graduated from the University of Georgia and joined the King & Spalding law firm in 1918. He became one of the top attorneys with the firm and represented major Atlanta companies, including Georgia Power, Coca-Cola and Equitable Life Insurance. He became friends with Robert Woodruff, the president of the Coca-Cola Company, and he hired Sibley to become associate general counsel for Coca-Cola; he later became general counsel in 1935.

In 1946, Sibley became chairman of the board at Trust Company of Georgia, a leading bank with locations throughout the Southeast. For over fifteen years, Sibley helped the bank grow to one of the South's leading financial institutions. Later, when his father stepped down from the Coca-Cola board in 1979, Sibley was elected to that board as well, serving as director until 1991.

He was involved with many philanthropic organizations and educational institutions, including Berry Schools, Egleston Children Hospital and other community and civic projects. When he retired from the bank in 1959, he was one of the most respected men in the state.

In 1954, the Supreme Court ruled that segregation based on race in public schools was unconstitutional. The court's decision in *Brown v. the Board of Education* marked a turning point in race relations in the United States and made equal opportunity in education the law of the land. Georgia, along with other southern states, fought the change, and in 1956, Georgia

John Sibley. *Atlanta History Center.*

Governor Marvin Griffin changed the state flag to include the Confederate Stars and Bars battle emblem. Governor Griffin asked the state legislature to endorse the change as a massive resistance to denounce the Supreme Court ruling. Griffin supported a state law that cut off state funds to any integrated public schools.

In 1960, many progressive leaders in Georgia wondered how to support the Supreme Court's decision against desegregation. Because of his reputation, Sibley was asked by the state legislature to head a special commission—the Sibley Commission—to sound out citizens concerned about efforts to integrate public schools. The committee crisscrossed the state and held public hearings on the issue. Sibley explained to more than eighteen thousand people who attended the hearings that the time had come for Georgians to accept the changes the court required.

The popular opinion was that Georgians were radical segregationists opposing any efforts allowing Black people their rightful, proper education. But Sibley rejected that idea. He believed that most Georgians agreed with the court's decision and wanted to choose compliance rather than the "separate but equal" policies of the past.

At the end of the public comments process, the Sibley Commission recommended that the state permit local school districts to decide for themselves whether to close or integrate. As a result, the legislature voted to end the law that would have cut off state funds to schools. Governor Ernest Vandiver signed a new law that gave him the power to decide future actions that allowed public schools to stay open.

The Sibley Commission helped keep Georgia's schools from closing during desegregation. Because of his efforts, Sibley became an inspiration to leaders of the civil rights movement, which defined rights for all Americans. He died in 1986 at the age of ninety-eight, a hero of his race and all races of Americans.

Sources

Basher, Barbara. John A. Sibley obituary. *New York Times*, October 27, 1986, section B, 8. www.nytimes.com.

Sibley, John A. Papers, Collection 437, Stuart A. Rose Archives, Emory Libraries. www.libraries.emory.edu.

B. FRANKLIN "FRANK" SKINNER IV

A GREAT CORPORATE CITIZEN
NOVEMBER 4, 1931–NOVEMBER 6, 2018

Benjamin Franklin Skinner was an example of a great corporate citizen. He believed in community service and was an inspiration to others who wanted to make a difference in people's lives. He was born in Covington, Virginia, and his father was Reverend Frank Skinner, who impressed upon him an obligation to help people, focusing primarily on children in need.

After graduating from the University of Richmond, Skinner's first job was with the local telephone company—the Chesapeake and Potomac Telephone Company of Virginia—which began a forty-year career in the telecommunication industry. He took assignments in Washington, D.C., Charlotte, Miami and Atlanta, where he was named president of Southern Bell, the largest telephone company in the Southeast.

He served as chairman of the board of the Atlanta Chamber of Commerce and served on the chambers' boards in each city in which he lived. Skinner also served as chairman of the board of Central Atlanta Progress and as a trustee of the Metropolitan Atlanta Community Foundation. He chaired the United Negro College Fund Campaign and was president of the Rotary Club and general chairman of the United Way.

He became a trustee of several colleges and universities, including Morehouse College in Atlanta, Davidson College, the University of Richmond and Columbia Theological Seminary. Skinner served on the boards of Nations Bank (now Bank of America), the Barclays American Corporation and other companies.

Skinner received multiple awards for public service, including the Lifetime Achievement Award of Christian and Jews and the Blanchard Award for

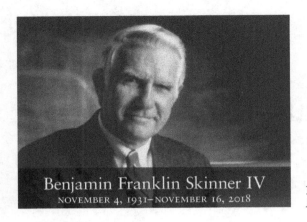

Benjamin Franklin Skinner IV
NOVEMBER 4, 1931–NOVEMBER 16, 2018

B. Franklin "Frank" Skinner IV.
Rotary Club of Atlanta.

Ethical Leadership. He was named one of *Georgia Trend* magazine's One Hundred Most Influential Georgians and admitted to the Hall of Fame of Influential Georgians.

His involvement with the Salvation Army was his major love; he was chairman of the national board of directors. He was honored as a life member in the organization and inducted into the army's Order of Distinguished Auxiliary Service.

In April 1995, tragedy struck when Franklin invited the Salvation Army board to his home. During the reception, the deck of his home collapsed, injuring many people in attendance, including Skinner. He sustained a fractured pelvis but insisted that all those injured should be taken to the hospital to receive medical care. He was the last person to receive treatment. Because of his role in the event, Skinner received the Others Award, the highest honor given to a National Salvation Army volunteer.

Skinner later became CEO of BellSouth Telecommunication and retired in 1992. He maintained his involvement in many other civic organizations and always gave his time and commitment to help his fellow man. He died of Parkinson's disease in 2018 and was best known for being a person who was the example of the Salvation Army's mission of "Neighbors Helping Others."

Sources

Atlanta Journal-Constitution. "Benjamin Franklin Skinner IV, 1931–2018." November 19, 2018. www.legacy.com.

Saporta, Maria. "Atlanta Civic Leader Frank Skinner—A Giant of a Human Being—Passes Away." *Atlanta Business Chronicle*, November 19, 2018. bizjournals.com.

GOVERNOR JOHN "JACK" M. SLATON

THE GOVERNOR WHO TRIED TO SAVE THE LIFE
OF LEO FRANK
DECEMBER 25, 1866–JANUARY 11, 1955

S laton was born in Meriwether County and graduated from the University of Georgia. He became an attorney in Atlanta and served in the Georgia legislature before being appointed governor of Georgia in 1911, later being elected for a full term in 1912. As governor, Slaton was known in history as the man who commuted the sentenced Leo Frank from death to life. He took courageous action in advancing civil rights for Jews and people of color.

In the early part of the twentieth century, Georgia, like other southern states, was known as a bigoted, racist and dangerous place for people of color. This image was highlighted in 1915 by the Leo Frank case, in which a Jewish man in Atlanta was placed on trial and convicted of raping and murdering a thirteen-year-old girl named Mary Phagan.

On April 26, 1913, Leo Max Frank spent the morning in his office of the National Pencil Factory working on his books. Employee Mary Phagan came to his office and asked for her pay, and Frank gave her a paycheck. Mary's body was found at the rear of the factory's basement around 3:30 p.m. At first, the police arrested the Black night watchman, who discovered the body. But after the police investigated the crime, they determined that Frank was the killer. He was arrested and charged with the murder.

The event became a media sensation. Local newspapers took pictures of the body and placed it on the front page with ghoulishly titillating headlines. One local Atlanta newspaper, the *Jefferson*, was published by racist Tom Watson, who pushed the jury to find Frank guilty as charged. The

Governor John "Jack" M. Slaton.
Atlanta History Center.

Jefferson ran headlines each day of the trial portraying Frank as a lewd, loathsome Jew. Other newspapers, including the *Atlanta Journal* and the *Atlanta Constitution*, were more moderate. Soon, the story attracted national headlines from the *New York Times* and William Randolph Hearst newspapers located all over the United States.

Frank was found guilty and sentenced to hang. Newspapers across the country condemned the jury. They said an innocent man had been sentenced to death because of clamor from a community that seemed to have gone mad through passion and prejudice.

Governor John M. Slaton examined the evidence and decided there was no proof of guilt. He changed the sentence from death to life in prison. His decision enraged people, and rioting broke out throughout the state. A mob threatened to storm the Slaton home in Atlanta and attack him and his family. The governor declared martial law and called out the National Guard to keep matters from getting out of control.

On the night of August 17, a mob from Mary's hometown took Leo Frank from his cell in Milledgeville, drove him to Marietta and hanged him from an oak tree. Frank's lynching was highly publicized and exposed the world to Georgia's shameful treatment of Jews, Blacks and other minorities.

Fearing for his family, Slaton fled the state and stayed away for ten years before he felt it was safe to return. He rejoined his old law firm and practiced law for the next forty years, but he was never elected to any state office again.

Sources

Oney, Steve. *And the Dead Shall Rise: The Murder of Mary Phagan and the Lynching of Leo Frank.* New York: Pantheon Books, 2003.

Woodward, C. Van. *Tom Watson, Agrarian Rebel.* Savannah, GA: Beehive Press, 1938. Repr., 1973.

LOUISE SUGGS

ONE OF GOLF'S GREAT CHAMPIONS
SEPTEMBER 7, 1923–AUGUST 7, 2015

Louise Suggs was a great golfer who won sixty-one career tournaments. She was the co-founder and first president of the Ladies Professional Golf Association (LPGA).

Louise was a native of Atlanta and grew up playing golf on a small golf course located in Lithia Springs, a community outside Atlanta. In her early teens, she started playing in women's amateur tournaments. Over the next few years, she won matches in amateur events, including the Georgia State Amateur Championship, the Southern Amateur Championship, the Women's North-South Tournament and the U.S. Women's Amateur Championship in 1947. She was only twenty-five years old when she won the British Amateur Championship in 1948.

That same year, Suggs turned professional and, along with Babe Didrikson Zaharias and Phyllis Otto, became one of the big three in women's golf. Suggs was known for her salty personality and speaking her mind. She felt she could outplay many of the men on their tournament events. Her car license plate read "TEED OFF."

In 1950, Suggs and twelve other female golfers created the LPGA. The group organized fourteen successful professional golf tournaments all over the country with $50,000 in prize money. Today, the tour encompasses thirty-two tournaments with purses close to $60 million. One of the organization's goals is encouraging other women to play professional golf, and in 1959, the association created the T&CP, its Teaching and Club Professional division. The T&CP now has a membership of 1,800 golf teachers, golfers, facility

Louise Suggs. *Carl E. Linde/AP/Shutterstock.*

managers and coaches. The LPGA is one of the most successful professional organizations in the world.

Suggs had fifty-eight LPGA career wins and won eleven major championships. In 1957, she won the Vare Trophy (for low scoring average). Suggs also became the first player in the LPGA to complete the career grand slam, winning the U.S. Women's Open, the LPGA Championship, the Western Open and the Titleholders Championship, at that time.

Over the years, she has been honored with many awards, including being inducted into the LPGA Hall of Fame and the World Golf Hall of Fame and winning the Bobby Jones Award for "distinguished sportsmanship in golf." In 2000, the LPGA created the Louise Suggs Trophy, presented annually to the Rolex Rookie of the Year.

Suggs retired from professional golf in 1962 but played on tour for many years. She was disappointed that the money awards became higher than they had been in her early playing years. She publicly declared when one tournament awarded $983,922 to the winner that "I wish like hell I could have played for this kind of money, but if not for me, they wouldn't be playing for playing for it, either."

Into her seventies, Suggs taught golf to people using local golf clubs, including Sea Island Golf and Country Club at St. Simons Island. In one of her most memorable quotes, she said, "Golf is very much like a love affair. If you don't take it seriously, it's not fun. But if you do, it breaks your heart. Don't break your heart, but flirt with the possibility."

Sources

Britannica. "Louise Suggs, American Golfer." www.britannica.com.

Legacy. "Louise Suggs obituary." www.legacy.com.

LPGA. "Louise Suggs, Co-founder of the Ladies Professional Golf Association (LPGA)." www.lpga.com/players/louise-suggs/81922/bio.

Suggs, Louise. *Golf for Women*. New York: Doubleday Company, 1960.

Suggs, Louise, and Elaine Scott. *And That's That! The Life Story of One of Golf's Great Champions*. Bloomington, IN: AuthorHouse, 2014.

DAN SWEAT

WON THE SHINING LIGHT AWARD FOR PUBLIC SERVICE
DECEMBER 21, 1933–FEBRUARY 28, 1997

Dan Sweat was Atlanta's premier civic administrator who linked public policy with humanity for all citizens. He held no political office but became a force in the planning and development of the city of Atlanta. He worked with mayors and governors and later in his career teamed with former president Jimmy Carter to head the Atlanta Project, designed to deal with poverty in many areas of the city.

Sweat was born in Waycross and came to Atlanta after graduating from high school. He served in the military and graduated from Georgia State College (now Georgia State University) with a degree in public administration. He worked as a reporter at the *Atlanta Journal* before moving to the city as an aide to Mayor Ivan Allen Jr. He later became the city's chief administrative officer. In 1970, Sweat kept this same post when Mayor Sam Massell was elected.

When the diminutive Massell came to his new office, he directed Sweat to find him a new desk because Massell was too short to see over it. Sweat proved his skill as an administrator. Instead of ordering a new desk, Sweat and his aide, George Berry, took a saw and cut the legs off. The next day, when Massell sat at what he thought was the new desk, he commended Sweat for doing a good job. Massell never knew he was sitting at the same desk.

Sweat went on to head the Atlanta Regional Commission and then had a fifteen-year career as president of Central Atlanta Progress, an association

Atlanta at night. *David Tulis/UPI/Shutterstock.*

of downtown business leaders. He was known for cutting through the red tape that angered many city officials, including Mayor Maynard Jackson.

He was credited with rescuing the Chattahoochee River and the water supply coming to Atlanta. He transformed a large, abandoned tract of land downtown, turning it into a mixed-income community for Black and white residents.

He left Central Atlanta Progress and teamed with businessman Tom Cousins to head up the Cousins Foundation, which in part focused on helping children and breaking the cycle of poverty. In 1991, former president Jimmy Carter hired him to run the Atlanta Project, a massive effort to pull together business, civic and community groups to solve urban problems.

During his career, he recruited many public administrators that were part of "Dan's Army." He trained many, and his protégés became heads of civic organizations like the Atlanta Chamber of Commerce and the Community Foundation for Greater Atlanta.

Sweat received numerous awards, including the WSB Radio/Atlanta Gas Light Co. Shining Light Award and the Leadership Georgia's J.W. Fanning Fellow Award, presented by the University of Georgia.

Sweat died in Atlanta in 1997. He was known as a man who dedicated himself to building a city where Black and white people could work together to build compassion and community.

Sources

Georgia State University, Andrew Young School of Policy Studies. "Dan E. Sweat Biography." aysps.gsu.edu/public-management-policy/dan-e-sweat-biography.

Thomas, Robert. "Dan Sweat Dies at 63, Guided Atlanta." *New York Times*, March 9, 1997.

GOVERNOR EUGENE TALMADGE

"YES, I STOLE, BUT I STOLE FOR YOU,
THE PEOPLE OF GEORGIA"
SEPTEMBER 23, 1884–DECEMBER 21, 1946

Eugene Talmadge was governor of Georgia for three terms, and he dominated politics during the 1930s and 1940s. He actively ran for office on a platform that promoted segregation and white supremacy.

Talmadge was born in Forsyth. He attended the University of Georgia, where he graduated with a law degree. He set up his law practice in Montgomery County, later moving to a farm in Telfair County. He was soon elected state agriculture commissioner in 1926.

During his term, Talmadge developed a reputation as a man who disregarded ethics and ruled his office in a corrupt manner. Talmadge was accused of pocketing $20,000 (more than $300,000 in today's dollars) with an order that raised the price of hogs. When the *Atlanta Journal* exposed his crooked actions, he famously told people all over the state, "Sure I stole it! But I stole it for you."

In 1932, he ran for governor on a platform of segregation, limited government and low taxes. At the time, the county unit system gave power to rural communities. Each small county had the same number of electoral votes as the large counties. Talmadge easily won the election because his popular base was in small communities where he told people that he was the poor man's friend.

Talmadge was a colorful character and campaigned by visiting every county courthouse, drawing large crowds. He wore red suspenders and a straw hat, taking on "the rich Atlanta elite" and "those lying Atlanta newspapers." The public loved his speeches and screamed, "Give 'em hell, Gene!"

Governor Eugene Talmadge. *AP/Shutterstock.*

As governor, he continued his corrupt ways on a higher level. His favorite control method was to call martial law against any state agency that failed to do his bidding. When the state Department of Transportation defied his requests, he fired the board members and installed his own people. When the state treasurer and comptroller general refused his orders, he had the state police remove them from office.

Over the years, Talmadge kept getting elected and became a virtual dictator. He ran and won in 1932 and 1934. He ran again in 1940 on a platform supporting racism and segregation. Because of the county unit voting system, people kept electing him because they felt he was a friend to the common man.

When the University of Georgia dean, Walter Cocking, advocated bringing Black students to the college, Talmadge called the Georgia Board of Regents to remove Cocking. The regents refused because they were a separate agency protected from the governor's control. Talmadge restructured the board and put in his people as replacements. The new board then fired Dean Cocking and others who went against the governor's orders. The Southern Association of Colleges removed accreditation from all Georgia state universities at the end of 1941, making students' degrees worthless.

Mainly because of the university controversy, Talmadge lost his bid for reelection in 1942 to Ellis Arnall. (Accreditation was restored in 1942, after Arnall became governor.) He ran again during the election in 1946 and promised he would restore a closed white primary election that excluded Black people from the voting process. He lost the popular vote to moderate James V. Carmichael but won on the county unit vote. It was his fourth victory in which he managed to use the unit system to secure the state's highest office.

There was a story that Talmadge called a local election official in one Georgia county and asked him, "How many people have voted for me?" The election official was a Talmadge supporter and replied, "How many do you need, Gene?"

In December 1946, before he could be sworn into office for a fourth term, Talmadge died. Nevertheless, he still tried to control the election. In his will, he insisted that his son, Herman, take over in his place. His death precipitated the 1947 "Three Governors Controversy," making Georgia a laughingstock to the rest of the nation. No fewer than three men claimed the governorship: Herman Talmadge, Ellis Arnall (the outgoing governor) and Melvin E. Thompson (the newly elected lieutenant governor).

On January 15, the day the legislature planned to take action, both Herman Talmadge and Arnall claimed that they were governor. They shared the same offices in the capitol, and the next day, Talmadge seized the office and changed the locks on the door. Arnall set up a satellite office at an information kiosk but eventually gave up his claim as governor and supported Thompson.

An *Atlanta Journal* reporter named George Goodwin found voting fraud in Talmadge's home in Telfair County. Goodwin found that some people rose from their graves and were counted and voted for Gene's son Herman. It appeared impossible that thirty-four citizens could have appeared at the polls and voted in alphabetical order, starting with the first letter and stopping abruptly at *K*. Goodwin won the Pulitzer Prize for exposing Talmadge's crooked effort to change the election even after his death.

In March 1947, after two months of haggling, the Georgia Supreme Court finally ruled that the duly elected lieutenant governor, Marvin E. Thompson, was Eugene Talmadge's successor He served through 1948, when he was defeated in a special election by Herman Talmadge.

Sources

Anderson, William. *The Wild Man from Sugar Creek: The Political Career of Eugene Talmadge*. Baton Rouge: Louisiana State University Press, 1975.

Cook, James F. *Carl Sanders: Spokesman of the New South*. Macon, GA: Mercer University Press, 1993.

Pomerantz, Gary M. *Where Peachtree Meets Sweet Auburn: A Saga of Race and Family*. New York: Penguin Books, 1996.

Talmadge, Herman E., and Mark Royden Winchell. *Talmadge: A Political Legacy, a Political Life*. Atlanta: Peachtree Press, 1987.

GOVERNOR HERMAN TALMADGE

"NOT WHERE I COME FROM!"
AUGUST 9, 1913–MARCH 21, 2002

Herman Talmadge was born in McRae in Telfair County. He was the son of Eugene "Gene" Talmadge, who served as governor in the 1930s and 1940s. After his father dominated politics during that era, his son continued the family dynasty by serving as Georgia's governor from 1948 to 1955 and in the U.S. Senate beginning in 1956 and for the next twenty-five years.

Talmadge continued his father's legacy of being a foe of civil rights for Black people and carrying on other discriminatory practices. In 1954, the United States Supreme Court ruled on *Brown v. the Board of Education*, stating that segregated public schools were unconstitutional. As governor, and later as Senator Talmadge, he remained a supporter of racial segregation, even after the Civil Rights Act of 1964.

During his years in the Senate, Talmadge gained the chairmanship of the powerful Senate Agriculture and Forestry Committee. He was a sponsor of the bill that created the food stamp program to help the poor but also his rural farming constituents. He also advocated provisions within the bill that able-bodied recipients must work for benefits. He protected Georgia's peanut farmers by helping establish price control programs on agricultural commodities.

In 1973, he gained national attention when he was appointed to the Senate Watergate Committee investigating the illegal activities of the Nixon administration. His colorful southern speech was well received by the general

Herman Talmadge. *Library of Congress.*

public, and his questions to White House officials were pointed and direct. He asked Nixon's chief of staff, H.R. Haldeman, why Nixon approved the wiretapping of private citizens' phones. Talmadge asked Haldeman whether he believed that a man's home is his castle. When he said he considered that an old-fashioned concept, Talmadge told him it wasn't "where I come from." Talmadge became a national figure for his comments during the committee proceedings.

Talmadge was popular and believed in being responsive to local citizens. He was one of the longest-serving political figures in Georgia. He loved to criticize Washington's bigwig policies and complain that the United States should not be the "Santa Claus of the whole world."

In 1979, he became involved in a scandal by improperly accepting government reimbursements of $43,435.82 for personal expenses. The U.S. Senate censured Talmadge for this and other improper financial actions.

Talmadge filed for divorce from his wife, Betty, in 1977. She contested the action, and during the trial, she accused Talmadge of cruel treatment and brought up his drinking troubles. His wife said that Talmadge had an overcoat with pockets full of cash from illegal political contributions. She won a large settlement and land, including their home in Lovejoy.

The censure by the Senate and his divorce effectively ended his political career and his public reputation. Republican Mack Mattingly defeated Talmadge in his last campaign. After the loss to Mattingly, Talmadge retired and lived another twenty years.

Sources

Cook, James F. *Carl Sanders: Spokesman of the New South*. Macon, GA: Mercer University Press, 1993.

Pomerantz, Gary M. *Where Peachtree Meets Sweet Auburn: A Saga of Race and Family*. New York: Penguin Books, 1996.

Talmadge, Herman E., and Mark Royden Winchell. *Talmadge: A Political Legacy, a Political Life*. Atlanta: Peachtree Press, 1987.

JUSTICE CLARENCE THOMAS

HE PROVES HIS CONSERVATIVE VALUES
JUNE 23, 1948-

United States Supreme Court justice Clarence Thomas is the first Georgian to be named to the highest court in the land. Thomas was only the second Black member of the court, after Thurgood Marshall, whose seat he filled.

Known for his conservative views, Thomas believes that government should play a smaller role in regulating personal liberty and that traditional American values should be preserved in the Constitution. President George H.W. Bush nominated Thomas, but he faced a difficult Senate confirmation because of his conservative views and a sexual harassment charge from lawyer Anita Hill.

Thomas was born near Savannah in the small community of Pin Point, near the Savannah River. He was raised by devoutly Catholic grandparents, intending to become a priest. He went to a Black Catholic high school and seminary prep school. He went to seminary but left after hearing a classmate celebrate the murder of Dr. Martin Luther King Jr. He enrolled at Holy Cross College, graduating with an honors degree in English in 1971. That fall, he began law school at Yale, specializing in business. He graduated in 1974.

He was admitted to the Missouri Bar and started his legal career as assistant attorney general for the state. After leaving government service, he was an attorney for the Monsanto Company and moved to Washington, becoming a legislative assistant to Senator John C. Danforth of Missouri.

Clarence Thomas. *J. Scott Applewhite/AP/ Shutterstock.*

In 1980, Thomas was appointed assistant secretary for civil rights in the Department of Education. The next year, he was named chairman of the United States Equal Employment Opportunity Commission (EEOC). President George H.W. Bush appointed him to the United States Court of Appeals for the District of Columbia Circuit in 1990. The following year, President Bush nominated Thomas to the Supreme Court of the United States. The Senate confirmed the appointment on October 15, 1991.

His nomination was controversial and attracted national media attention. During the hearings, a former EEOC employee, Anita Hill, testified that Thomas used his position to humiliate her during her employment. She claimed that Thomas repeatedly made sexually inappropriate comments, which constituted sexual harassment and workplace harassment.

Thomas denied the allegations and stated that his critics were using Hill to attack his conservative positions on abortion rights, civil rights and other liberal causes. With the nation watching, he called the hearing "a high-tech lynching for uppity Blacks who in any way deign to think for themselves." Thomas was approved by the Senate when the committee decided that there was no evidence to prove Hill's claims.

During his time on the court, Thomas has proven his conservative values. He is known for having a quiet demeanor during the court's oral arguments and asking few questions. His court decisions follow the principle of laws of "originalism," a concept that the interpretation of laws in the Constitution should be interpreted on their original understanding "at their time" they were written.

Thomas's conservative values influence many of his decisions. For example, he has been against affirmation action in colleges and universities, despite qualifying for and benefiting from the program. (Thomas attended Yale Law School thanks to affirmative action quotas.) He dissented in the Supreme Court landmark decision to uphold the constitutional rights of gay couples to get married in 2015. He also dissented on the court's decision to maintain federal tax subsidies of the Affordable Care Act.

Thomas lives in Washington, D.C., with his wife, Virginia Lamp. In 2007, he wrote a memoir, *My Grandfather's Son*.

Sources

Biography. "Clarence Thomas." www.biography.com.
Supreme Court of the United States. "Clarence Thomas." www.supremecourt.gov.
Thomas, Clarence. *My Grandfather's Son: A Memoir*. New York: Harper Perennial, 2007.

TED TURNER

CAPTAIN OUTRAGEOUS BUILT A MEDIA EMPIRE
NOVEMBER 19, 1938–

T ed Turner is the most outrageous person to be included in this list. The hyperkinetic billionaire is responsible for, among many other things, the first national cable station (dubbed a "Superstation") and launching the first global television news network, CNN.

Early in his life, Turner experienced signs of mania. His risk-taking life is best explained by an incident that occurred when he was a teenager. Racing his first car down a road, Turner saw a train moving down the track faster. He thought he could drive at ninety miles an hour to beat the train across the tracks. He flew across the tracks, losing control of the car and grazing the locomotive by an inch. A man driving near him wondered why anyone would be so careless. Another bystander responded, "That must be Ted Turner. He always drives that way!"

When Ted was growing up in Savannah, his father was an abusive parent who demeaned him and gave his son the feeling that he would be a failure. After attending college at Brown University (he didn't graduate), Turner came back home to join Turner Advertising, his family's regional outdoor advertising business. His father died in 1963, leaving the business deeply in debt. When Turner became president, he was able to work out new financial arrangements, and under his leadership, the company went from a small local business to a billion-dollar enterprise.

He grew the Savannah operation by buying other outdoor advertising companies in several states. One company included several radio stations, so Turner became interested in radio and expanded, buying more stations. In 1970, he took a giant leap with the purchase of a UHF television station.

Ted Turner. *Jennifer Stalcup Photography*.

Turner saw an opportunity to use the satellite to transmit television programs directly to cable companies all over the United States.

His new company was called the Turner Broadcasting System. He broadcast old movies and classic television shows on his "Superstation" to entertain viewers. In 1976, he purchased the Atlanta Braves to guarantee sports programming for his burgeoning television empire. As the business grew, he bought MGM's movie library. He created TNT and Turner Classic Movies, bringing in even more viewers by offering Academy Award–winning titles and classics like *The Wizard of Oz* and *Casablanca*. In 1991, Turner bought Hanna-Barbera Cartoons, allowing him to create the Cartoon Network.

But Turner's manic personality gave him little time for his family. He was working eighteen hours a day; he spent his off time at Braves games. His antics caused him to become an eccentric and well-known figure both in Atlanta and across the nation. At one Braves opening day, Turner took the mound in a Braves uniform and threw the first pitch. The fans loved it.

He purchased the Atlanta Hawks NBA team. He also ventured into competitive sailing, winning the America Cup with the yacht *Courageous* in 1977. But his drunken acceptance speech at the awards ceremony and other controversial statements and actions earned him the nickname "Captain Outrageous" and "The Mouth of the South."

His empire was awash in debt, with interest payments higher than revenues. He visited his friend Tom Cousins to ask for a $1 million loan to help make his monthly payroll. As he was leaving, Cousins asked him what he would be doing next. There were only three national news television networks at the time: ABC, CBS and NBC.

Turner replied, "I'm going to put all of them out of business. I am going to create a news television network that will provide twenty-four-hour news coverage all over the world." When Turner left, Cousins commented, "I just gave $1 million to a crazy man!"

Turner began his new venture in 1980, calling it the Cable News Network, or CNN. He started it on a shoestring, selling one of his television channels for seed money. Many of his executives at the Turner Broadcasting System home office in Atlanta were afraid his new venture would bankrupt the company. At the time, no one thought a worldwide all-news, all-the-time network could make it. Turner planned to have a bureau in every major city globally, and many of his staff thought the goal was financially infeasible.

But Turner forged ahead, hiring several rival network top executives and journalists, including veteran journalist Daniel Schorr, to give CNN credibility. Turner believed that audiences wanted a platform where they could find information whenever they wanted. Now, almost forty years later, CNN is worth about $5 billion. Not bad for a $20 million initial investment.

In 1996, the media giant Time Warner acquired Turner Broadcasting System for $7.5 billion. Time Warner then merged with the Internet company America Online (AOL) in 2001. Ted Turner was named vice chairman of the new company, and his personal assets grew to over $10 billion. The merger was a failure, Turner left the company and his net worth dropped to $2.5 billion.

Among Turner's many accomplishments include establishing the Turner Foundation with a vision for conservation of environmental causes throughout the world (1990) and buying the 578,000-acre Vermejo Park Ranch in New Mexico and, with other future land purchases, becoming the second-largest landowner in North America. He raises fifty-one thousand bison, which stocks his restaurant chain, Ted's Montana Grill (1996). He also pledged $1 billion to the United Nations (1997) and established the Nuclear Threat Initiative with former Georgia senator Sam Nunn (2001).

He is considered a significant philanthropist and has joined Warren Buffet's Giving Pledge, vowing to donate virtually all of his wealth to charity by the time of his death. Ever the risk-taker, Turner is an incredibly successful businessman who demonstrates outstanding leadership ability. He has also mentored many people who followed his leadership style and became prominent business executives in the television industry.

Sources

Bibb, Porter. *Ted Turner: It Ain't as Easy as It Looks*. Boulder, CO: Johnson Books, 1993.

Roth, Michael S. "Review of *Call Me Ted*, by Ted Turner." *San Francisco Chronicle*, November 9, 2012. sfgate.com.

Turner, Ted, and Bill Burke. *Call Me Ted*. New York: Grand Central Publishing, 2008.

GOVERNOR ERNEST VANDIVER

GEORGIA'S MOST FAMOUS GOVERNOR
JULY 3, 1918–FEBRUARY 21, 2005

E rnest Vandiver was born near Lavonia and became one of the most famous governors in Georgia's recent history. In 1961, he forced the desegregation of the University of Georgia and all Georgia public schools despite strong pro-segregation views from white voters. He ran on a platform of keeping Black people out of the school system, pledging, "No, not one!" After he was elected governor, he reversed his stand, committing political suicide by his action. He was never reelected to any office in the future.

Vandiver was educated in Lavonia Public Schools and the Darlington School in Rome, Georgia, and graduated from the University of Georgia. After college, he moved back to Lavonia, married and became mayor of the city. He became a supporter of political figures, including Herman Talmadge, and supported his successful Senate race. With Talmadge's help, Vandiver ran for lieutenant governor successfully in 1954. He ran for governor in 1958 and won by one of the broadest margins in Georgia history.

Vandiver became friends with many national political figures of the day, including future president John F. Kennedy. He endorsed the Kennedy-Johnson presidential ticket and helped win Georgia voters in the general election of 1960. When civil rights leader Martin Luther King Jr. was jailed in DeKalb County for a trumped-up traffic ticket violation, United States attorney general Robert Kennedy made a call asking the newly elected governor to intervene. Vandiver quietly made calls to local enforcement officials and judges to help overrule the sentence.

Ernest Vandiver. *AP/Shutterstock.*

In 1962, the U.S. Supreme Court declared Georgia's county unit system illegal. The county unit system gave equal voting power to each county with little regard for population differences. It also allowed rural white counties to reduce the impact of growing urban areas where most of the Black voters lived.

Vandiver changed the law, enabling the fair distribution of votes between Georgia's rural and urban areas. He also gave voters the principle of "one man, one vote." According to historians, the change was the most momentous political decision of the century in Georgia. Vandiver became very unpopular with white voters because of the change.

In 1961, Federal Judge William A. Bootle ordered the University of Georgia's desegregation when two Black students, Charlayne Hunter and Hamilton Holmes, applied for admission. Georgia's white power faction was furious and put pressure on Vandiver to have the state oppose the ruling. Other southern states passed laws that tried to overrun federal courts and keep pro-segregation, separate-but-equal laws in place.

During a special session in the state legislature, Vandiver was able to deal with the crisis. The state assembly's moderates passed a series of laws that gave Vandiver the power to desegregate the University of Georgia and all state schools. Charlayne Hunter and Hamilton Holmes soon enrolled in the university, and rabid pro-segregationists bitterly attacked Vandiver for his actions.

After his term as governor ended, Vandiver ran for U.S. Senate. But his policies ending segregation in schools and the county unit system made him deeply unpopular with rural voters. He came in third and found that his political career was over. He retired to his home in Lavonia, where he died at age eighty-six. The state named a part of I-85 near his home Ernest Vandiver Highway.

Sources

Henderson, Harold Paulk. "Ernest Vandiver." New Georgia Encyclopedia, August 12, 2002. www.georgiaencyclopedia.org.

Vandiver, Ernest, Jr. Papers, 1954–1998. Richard B. Russell Library, University of Georgia, Collection RBRL/186/SEV. www.libs.uga.edu.

CONGRESSMAN CARL VINSON

CHAMPION OF NAVAL MIGHT
AND MILITARY PREPAREDNESS
NOVEMBER 18, 1883–JUNE 1, 1981

During World War II, Congressman Carl Vinson was the "father of the two-ocean navy," and he is the only Georgia congressman to have a naval ship named for him. He was born in Baldwin County and graduated from Mercer University's law school in 1902. He was a judge in his native county when he ran for the U.S. Congressional Tenth District and was elected in 1914. At only thirty years old, he was the youngest member of Congress and served fifty years before retiring at age eighty-one.

He was a champion of naval affairs during World War I, World War II, the Korean Conflict and the Vietnam War. Vinson was chairman of the House Armed Services Committee, and admirals and generals called him the Swamp Fox because he grilled them on operations during committee hearings during the war years.

A few days after German troops conquered France, the Two-Ocean Navy Act increased the navy's size by 70 percent. The law was named for Carl Vinson and David Walsh, who chaired the Naval Affairs Committee in the House and Senate, respectively. The action increased the American combat fleet by 257 ships. Vinson's vision helped the United States become materially prepared when the Japanese attack on Pearl Harbor occurred, propelling the nation into war.

Following the end of the war, Vinson helped merge the Naval Affairs and Military Affairs Committees to become the House Armed Services Committee. He was named chairman of the new committee. He oversaw the military's modernization as it focused on the Cold War, which was the postwar geopolitical confrontation between the Soviet Union and the United States.

After his retirement in January 1964, the navy named a nuclear-powered aircraft carrier in his honor. At the launching ceremony in 1980, Vinson was in attendance when his grandnephew, Senator Sam Nunn, told the attendance, "Behind me is the mightiest naval warship ever constructed, the USS *Carl Vinson*. Beside me is a mighty and powerful figure in the history of our republic, Congressman Carl Vinson. It is fitting that this great vessel bear the name Carl Vinson, a name synonymous with military preparedness in the twentieth century." In 1964, President Lyndon Johnson awarded Vinson the President Medal of Freedom, the highest award the president can give to a civilian. In 1983, the University of Georgia renamed the Institute of Public Affairs the Carl Vinson Institute of Government.

Congressman Carl Vinson.
Library of Congress.

All of his friends called him "Admiral" when he retired to his farm in Milledgeville. He had married Mary Green in 1921. She died in 1949 after a long illness, and he never remarried. They had no children. In Milledgeville, he lived a life as a gentleman farmer until he passed away at age ninety-seven.

Sources

Congressional Record. "I Served with Great Uncle of Carl Vinson." Senator Sam Nunn. www.govinfo.gov.

History. "Congressman Carl Vinson, United States House of Representatives." Arts and Archives. www.history.gov.

McElroy, Roland. *The Best President the Nation Never Had*. Macon, GA: Mercer University Press, 2017.

ALICE WALKER

AWARD-WINNING BLACK AUTHOR, POET AND ACTIVIST
FEBRUARY 9, 1944-

Author Alice Walker was born in Eatonton, a town that is the home of another famous author, Joel Chandler Harris. She is a novelist, short story writer, poet and social activist for women's rights and Black Lives Matter causes. She is most famous for writing the book *The Color Purple*, for which she won the National Book Award and the Pulitzer Prize in 1983.

Her parents were sharecroppers, and as a young girl, she helped with family chores, including picking cotton during the growing season. She was blinded in one eye by an accident when she was eight; her parents were too poor to afford a car and could not take her to the doctor. Her mother gave her a typewriter, and she started writing short stories and poetry. This handicap influenced her writing, and she became an astute observer of human interactions.

She received a scholarship to Spelman College in Atlanta and later attended Sarah Lawrence College in New York. After graduating in 1965, she moved to Mississippi, started a teaching job and began publishing short stories and essays. Walker's first novel was *The Third Life of Grange Copeland*, which described three generations of a Black family's experiences during the civil rights era, over sixty years. Walker continued to write poetry, and her short stories told of the abuse of African American citizens in the Deep South.

She moved to New York and later to California, where she wrote her most popular novel, *The Color Purple*, in 1982. The book tells the story of two Black women joined by their love for each other, the children they

Alice Walker. *Stephen Lovekin/Shutterstock.*

care for and the men who abuse them. In the first part of the book, the narrator, Celie, tells God that her father has raped her, and she is pregnant for the second time with his child. Celie is then forced to marry a man named Albert, who continually abuses her. Albert has a mistress named Shug, whom Celie befriends, thus beginning a lifetime of love between the women. Many other characters dart in and out of the novel. The rise of self-confidence and strength of the women and rage over their abuse bring the story to its conclusion.

The Color Purple won the Pulitzer Prize for Fiction in 1983, making Alice Walker the first Black woman to win the award. The work also won the National Book Award for Fiction and was made into an acclaimed movie, directed by Steven Spielberg, starring Danny Glover, Whoopi Goldberg and Oprah Winfrey, and was also a Broadway musical.

Walker is a feminist, advocating for human rights and people of color. She has written six novels, three collections of short stories, four children's books and many books of poetry. Her work has been translated into more than two dozen languages, and her books have sold more than fifteen million copies.

One of her most famous poems is titled "The World We Want Is Us":

> *It moves my heart to see you awakened faces;*
> *The look of "aha!"*
> *shining, finally, in*
> *so many*
> *wide-open eyes....*
> *...The world we want is on the way; Arundhati*
> *and now we*
> *are*
> *hearing her breathing.*
> *That world we want is Us; united; already moving*
> *into it.*

Walker lives in Mendocino, California, with Robert Allen, the former senior editor of the *Black Scholar*.

Sources

Georgia Writers Hall of Fame. "Alice Walker Honored." georgiawritershalloffame.org.

Poetry Foundation. "Alice Walker." www.poetryfoundation.org.

Walker, Alice. *The Color Purple*. New York: Penguin Books, 1982.

HERSCHEL WALKER

AWARD-WINNING RUNNING BACK, HELPED WIN
1980 NATIONAL CHAMPIONSHIP
MARCH 3, 1962–

There goes Herschel! There goes Herschel! There goes Herschel!" said Larry Munson, Georgia football's famous radio announcer, during Herschel Walker's first season as a Georgia Bulldog. Walker is a native of Wrightsville and became the most famous football player in Georgia history, helping UGA win the National Championship in 1980 and winning the Heisman Trophy in 1982. Walker left college in 1983 and started his professional football career playing with the New Jersey Generals before moving to the Dallas Cowboys.

Walker had a severe speech impediment growing up, but he fought back, building his confidence by working on his physical conditioning. By the time he was a teenager, he was doing one thousand pushups a day.

He ran over ten miles each day after school and proved his capabilities as a high school sports star in track, basketball and football. In his senior year, he led the Johnson County Trojans to the Georgia state football championship. When he graduated from high school, he was named valedictorian of his class.

His first game as a Georgia Bulldog was against Tennessee. Georgia was the overwhelming underdog and behind 15–2 in the middle of the third quarter. Georgia's coach, Vince Dooley, took a chance and decided to put Walker in the game, an unusual move because, at the time, freshmen were not supposed to play until their second year. Walker took over the game and became a legend to Bulldog fans forever.

Larry Munson described Walter's first touchdown to the radio audience in excitement: "We hand it off to Herschel, there's a hole...5...10...12, he's running all over people! Oh, you Herschel Walker! My God Almighty, he

Herschel Walker. *Atlanta History Center.*

ran over two men! They had him dead away inside the 9. Herschel Walker went 16 yards, my God, a freshman!" Walker ran for another touchdown, and Georgia won the game, 16–15, before 100,000 stunned Tennessee fans.

Walker helped the Bulldogs win the next eleven games by rushing for a record 1,616 yards and fifteen touchdowns. The Bulldogs were ranked number one in the nation and played Notre Dame in the Sugar Bowl. Walker dislocated his shoulder early in the game, but he went back on the field as if nothing happened. He ran for another record 150 yards and scored two touchdowns, helping the team to a 17–10 victory. At the end of the season, the Associated Press declared Georgia number one in the country.

Over three college years, Walker rushed for a record 5,259 yards, completed forty-nine touchdowns, helped his team to a record of 34-3 over three seasons and secured the 1982 Heisman Trophy. Sportswriters named him one of the top college running backs of all time, and in 1999, *Sports Illustrated* named him to its College Football Team of the Century. When a sportscaster asked him how he could run 5,259 yards without being tired, he told him, "It's not hard; that ball is not heavy." Fans wondered how he could be so strong and violent on the field yet be so mild-mannered in person after the game.

Walker turned professional in 1983, leaving college and signing with the U.S. Football League's New Jersey Generals because underclassmen were still ineligible to play in the NFL. In 1986, he signed a $5 million contract and joined the Dallas Cowboys.

In 1988, he became a one-man offense, played seven positions, rushed and caught passes and became just the tenth player in NFL history to amass more than two thousand combined yards in a single season.

Walker changed teams during his pro football career and played for the Minnesota Vikings, Philadelphia Eagles, New York Giants and had a second stint with the Dallas Cowboys before retiring at the end of the 1997 season. He rushed for 25,283 all-purpose yards, placing him first all-time on the NFL list and second among the NFL's all-time leaders in total yards at his retirement. He participated in mixed martial arts, track and field and even ballet in his post-football sporting life. He competed in the 1992 Winter Olympics in Albertville, France, as a member of the two-man U.S. bobsled team while still an active NFL player.

Since his retirement from sports, Walker founded Renaissance Man Foods, one of the largest minority-owned chicken businesses in the United States. He also owns other companies, including a drapery business and a promotions and advertising company that employs more than eight hundred people in the South.

Walker wrote a book, *Breaking Free: My Life with Dissociate Identity Disorder*. His condition, dissociative identity disorder (DID) or multiple personality disorder, is a mental process that produces a lack of connection in a person's feelings, actions, memories and sense of identity. In layman's terms, a person can have two or more personalities that are entirely different from each other. Walker was diagnosed with the condition in 2002.

In his book, Walker recalls an event where he held a gun to his head and played Russian roulette. He told another story about waking up and telling his wife he was going to kill her. The next morning, he had to tell his wife that he had no memory of his action.

There is no cure for DID, but patients can live normal lives with proper diagnosis and treatment. Walker wrote his story to encourage other people living with the same condition, hoping to show them and others that, even living with DID, it's possible to lead a successful life.

Sources

Digital Library of Georgia. "UGA 1980 National Championship Season." dlg.usg.edu.

Nelson, Jon. *A History of College Football in Georgia*. Charleston, SC: The History Press, 2012.

Paugh, Jeff. *Herschel Walker: From the Georgia Backwoods and the Heisman Trophy to the Pros*. New York: Random House Sports Library, 1983.

Smith, Loran, and Lewis Grizzard. *Glory! Glory!* Atlanta: Peachtree Publishers, 1983.

Walker, Herschel, Gary Brozek and Charlene Maxfield. *Breaking Free: My Life with Dissociative Identity Disorder*. New York: Simon and Schuster, 2008.

York, Kyle. "Herschel Walker (born 1962)." New Georgia Encyclopedia. www.georgiaencyclopedia.org.

THOMAS E. WATSON

GEORGIA POPULIST POLITICIAN AND MUCKRAKER
SEPTEMBER 5, 1856–SEPTEMBER 26, 1922

homas E. Watson was a populist Georgia political figure who lived in the early part of the twentieth century. A populist is a person who strives to appeal to average citizens who feel the established political elite disregards them.

He was an author of some note, writing a two-volume history of France and biographies of Napoleon, Thomas Jefferson and Andrew Jackson. He also wrote a novel titled *Bethany: A Story of the Old South*. He owned his own publishing company, the Jeffersonian Publishing Company, and produced a magazine and newspaper, the *Weekly Jeffersonian Magazine*.

He used his influence to further his political and social views by owning various newspapers and magazines. He wrote muckraking editorials against Blacks, Catholics and Jews. He is best known for his writings during Leo Frank's trial for the murder of Mary Phagan.

Frank was a Jewish man and the superintendent of the National Pencil Company, where thirteen-year-old Phagan worked. On April 26, 1913, Frank was working in his office when Phagan came to ask for her wages. Later that afternoon, a watchman discovered Phagan's body at the rear of the factory's basement. Initially, police suspected Phagan had been killed by the man who found her body, but soon their suspicions turned toward Frank. He was arrested and charged with the crime.

Watson's newspaper ran daily—and sensational—headlines about the trial, portraying Frank as a "lewd, loathsome Jew." The paper also urged the jury to find Frank guilty of the murder. Later, Watson's newspaper fanned the

Thomas E. Watson. *Atlanta History Center.*

flames of public opinion by inciting a vigilante mob to break into Frank's jail cell, bring him to Marietta and lynch him in front of a large crowd. In reaction to the Leo Frank lynching, William Simmons climbed Stone Mountain, near Atlanta, and burned three giant crosses, proclaiming it the reincarnation of the Ku Klux Klan.

Watson was elected to the U.S. House of Representatives and later the U.S. Senate. The Populists unsuccessfully advocated for Watson to be William Jennings Bryan's running mate. In Congress, he helped pass the Rural Free Delivery law requiring the post office to deliver mail to remote farm families.

He was a dominant figure in Georgia politics and helped elect other Georgia governors who held his racist views. In 1920, he was elected to the Senate, advocating a platform supporting populist causes, and continued his attacks against Blacks, Catholics and Jews. National condemnation of Watson did not change his attitude, and he advocated for the Ku Klux Klan to restore his vision of a white supremacist nation.

Sources

Oney, Steve. *And the Dead Shall Rise: The Murder of Mary Phagan and the Lynching of Leo Frank.* New York: Pantheon Books, 2003.

Pomerantz, Gary M. *Where Peachtree Meets Sweet Auburn: A Saga of Race and Family.* New York: Penguin Group, 1996.

Woodward, C. Van. *Tom Watson, Agrarian Rebel.* New York: Macmillan Company, 1938. Repr., Savannah, GA: Beehive Press, 1973.

CATHERINE EVANS WHITENER

FOUNDER OF THE CARPET INDUSTRY
AUGUST 10, 1880–JUNE 2, 1964

I n the early 1900s, a significant industry was created by none other than a twelve-year-old girl. Catherine Evans Whitener is credited with founding the tufted carpet industry located in and around Dalton.

When she was twelve, Catherine made her first tufted bedspreads and unique coverlets for her friends and family. She soon began selling the quilts out of her home and became so successful she hired neighbors and trained them to keep up with demand. The spreads were made with a tufted yarn fabric called chenille, a French word for "caterpillar," whose fur it supposedly resembles.

Dalton was a mountain community with poor soil for farming, so people needed another method to support their families. Highway 41 was a major road going through Dalton. Whitener sold her beautiful hand-tufted bedspreads to northern tourists driving to Florida.

Whitener's business expanded when she decided her bedspreads could be used for floor coverings. She made tufted carpets and thousands more tufted items. In 1917, she opened the Evans Manufacturing Company and turned it into a successful business that propelled tufted carpet into a $10 billion industry. Today, almost all carpets are tufted using her early techniques, and Dalton is still known as the Carpet Capital of the World.

Whitener also helped her neighbors in need. Her friend Dicksie Bandy was having a hard time with her farm, and Whitener gave her some bedspread patterns so she could tuft some colorful bedspreads of her own to sell. Bandy boarded a train up north and returned with six hundred orders, enough to allow her and her husband to launch their bedspread business. In 1948, the family turned the business over to their son Jack Bandy, and Bandy, with a few

Catherine Evans Whitener. *Bucky McCamy, from the Dalton, Georgia History Museum.*

friends, converted the bedspread operation into making tufted carpet. They named the company Coronet Industries, and it became one of the largest manufacturers of carpet in the United States. In 1970, electronics giant RCA bought Coronet for millions of dollars.

Another example of Whitener's heritage is the success of Shaw Industries, one of the largest carpet companies in the world. Shaw started as a dye finishing company in 1946, producing scatter rugs. In 1958, Robert "Bob" Shaw and his brother Clay Shaw acquired Philadelphia Carpet and merged its finishing operation into carpetmaking as its primary product. Less than twenty years later, Shaw was a $43 million company. By 1985, it had become a $500 million operation with five thousand employees, and by 1999, it had become one of America's largest corporations with billions in sales. Shaw also founded a new company called Engineered Floors.

In the last part of the twentieth century, there were more than three hundred carpet manufacturers located within fifty miles of the city of Dalton, all because of Catherine Evans Whitener and her bedspread business. Today, more than 90 percent of the functional carpet produced in the world is still made in the Dalton area.

Whitener died in 1964. As a rural artisan, she founded one of the United States' most successful industries. In 2001, she was inducted into the Georgia Women of Achievement Hall of Fame.

Sources

Chapman, Dan. "Bob Shaw, Carpet King." *Atlanta Journal-Constitution*, August 29, 2013. www.AJC.com.

Daily Citizen-News (Dalton, GA). "Catherine Evans Whitener Started the Carpet Industry in Dalton." www.dailycitizen.news.

Georgia Women of Achievement. "Catherine Evans Whitener, Nurse, Volunteer, Social Activist." www.georgiawomen.org.

Jones, Jamie. "Jack Bandy, a Carpet Industry Pioneer." *Daily Citizen-News.* www.dailycitizen.news.

Pare, Mike. "Bob Shaw: Engineered Floors." *Chattanooga Times Free Press*, April 1, 2018. www.timesfreepress.com.

ROBERT WOODRUFF

THE PAUSE THAT REFRESHES
DECEMBER 6, 1889–MARCH 7, 1985

In the early days of the twentieth century, a Columbus store pharmacist named John Pemberton invented a soda soft drink that the locals thought tasted great. He was told he should bottle it to sell. He named the drink Coca-Cola. Asa Griggs Candler bought the formula from Pemberton and formed a company to bottle and distribute statewide. Today, beverages created by the Coca-Cola Company are sold in over two hundred countries where thirsty consumers purchase 1.8 billion servings a day.

In 1919, a group of investors headed up by Ernest Woodruff purchased the company from Candler and soon named Woodruff's son Robert as president. Robert Woodruff went on to expand Coca-Cola, and from 1923 to 1955, under his leadership, it became the most famous cola drink in the world.

Robert Woodruff felt his life had been a failure. He had a string of disappointments after high school. He attended Georgia Tech but flunked out and attended Oxford College of Emory University for one term but soon left. He worked as a laborer at a foundry company, shoveling sand and working as a machinist's apprentice. A year later, he was fired. Woodruff accepted a job from his father but soon left after he disagreed with the company's direction.

However, Woodruff loved automobiles. He took a sales job with the White Motor Company and quickly rose to be vice president of sales. During World I, he joined the U.S. Ordnance Department and helped White Motor Company supply most of the vehicles to the U.S. military.

Robert Woodruff. *Atlanta History Center.*

After the war, he and his father reconciled, and Woodruff accepted the job as president of the Coca-Cola Company. Coke was a small operation when he took over, and he used his talents from being a car salesman to take Coke to higher sales in the United States. He increased advertising and marketing support and assisted fountain outlets in aggressively selling their product.

He suggested selling soda in a glass bottle with a design that's still in use today. Woodruff also introduced new concepts like a six-pack carton, which became the company's most effective marketing tool because each package included a message to purchase more Coke.

Woodruff coined some of the most memorable advertising slogans in history. "The Pause that Refreshes" appeared in magazines and newspapers in 1929 and defined Coca-Cola as a world leader. His vision brought the company to Europe, and it wasn't long before Coca-Cola expanded to the rest of the world.

Woodruff ran the company for more than thirty years and retired as president in 1955. He remained on the board of directors until 1984. Woodruff was a philanthropist and made significant contributions to Atlanta institutions, including Emory University, Georgia Tech, the Boy Scouts and other nonprofits. Before his death in 1985, he created the Robert W. Woodward Foundation, which continues his philanthropic legacy.

Sources

Allen, Fredrick. *Atlanta Rising*. Atlanta: Longstreet Press, 1996.
———. *Secret Formula: The Inside Story of How Coca-Cola Became the Best-Known Brand in the World*. New York: Open Road Integrated Media, 1994.
Young, Andrew, Harvey Newman and Andrea Young. *Andrew Young and the Making of Modern Atlanta*. Macon, GA: Mercer University Press, 2016.

COLLETT EVERMAN "C.E." WOOLMAN

DELTA: FROM CROP DUSTING
TO MAJOR WORLDWIDE AIRLINE
OCTOBER 8, 1889–SEPTEMBER 11, 1966

C ollett Woolman was the founder of Delta Air Lines, leading what started as the world's first crop-dusting business in 1925 to form one of the most successful scheduled airlines worldwide.

Woolman was born in Bloomington, Indiana, and attended the University of Illinois, graduating in 1912. Aviation was in the early stages of development, and Woolman became hooked on flight after attending the world's first airplane meet in Rheims, France.

Back in the United States, the boll weevil was threatening to destroy the South's cotton industry. Woolman saw an opportunity to help farmers combat the pest by dusting crops with calcium arsenate from the air. In 1925, Huff Daland Dusters hired Woolman as its chief entomologist and started commercial crop-dusting in Macon. It soon became so successful that it expanded, adding eighteen planes capable of dusting crops throughout the South.

The company moved to Monroe, Louisiana, and expanded operations to Peru in South America. The Peruvian government then awarded mail contracts to the company, which contracted with Pan-Am subsidiary to fly a six-passenger Fairchild airplane from Lima to Paiva and other cities.

Woolman returned to the United States and convinced a group of investors to buy Huff Daland Dusters, changing its name to Delta Air Service for the Mississippi Delta region it served. Woolman was named vice president in 1929 and named to the board of directors in 1930, and the company began passenger service to other cities, including routes that stretched from

C.E. Woolman. *Delta Air
Lines, Inc.*

Dallas, Texas, to Jackson, Mississippi. It kept its dusting operation and
started airmail contracts with the U.S. Postal Service, delivering mail from
Fort Worth, Texas, to Charleston, South Carolina.

In 1941, Delta moved to Atlanta. The airline continued its growth and
in 1953 merged with Chicago and Southern Airlines, giving it access to the
Great Lake region in the upper Midwest and points in the Caribbean Sea.
The company continued to grow through mergers and expansions. In 1945,
Woolman was named president and general manager of the company, later
chairman of the board and CEO in 1965.

Woolman preferred to live a simple life, shunning media attention. He
was modest about his charitable efforts, his church giving and his other gifts
to community nonprofits. He had a genuine concern for all his employees
and was famous for telling them to follow the golden rule by "doing to others
as you will do for yourself." He grew orchids as a hobby and would often
surprise his employees by giving them samples to take home.

His favorite quotes included, "Let us put ourselves on the other side of
the counter. We have a responsibility over and above the price of a ticket,"

"An employee's devotion to his or her company, dedication to the job and consideration for the customer determine a company's reputation" and "Always be considerate of your fellow employees."

On his twenty-fifth anniversary of being with Delta, his staff and employees presented him with a new Cadillac and a painting of himself "on behalf of the pilots of Delta, our wives, and children, in appreciation for what you have done for us and permitted us to do for ourselves."

Woolman died in 1996 at age seventy-seven. His biography on the Delta Museum website says that he was survived by his daughters, grandchildren "and a family of 13,000 Delta employees."

Sources

Jones, Geoff. *Delta Air Lines: 75 Years of Airline Excellence*. Charleston, SC: Arcadia Publishing, 2003.

National Aviation Hall of Fame. "Woolman, Collett, C.E., Entrepreneur, Enshrined in the National Business Aviation Association in 1994." nationalaviation.org.

ANDREW YOUNG

WALK IN MY SHOES
MARCH 12, 1932–

A ndrew Young was a significant figure in the civil rights movement of the 1960s. He later became mayor of Atlanta, a member of Congress and U.S. ambassador to the United Nations. Young worked closely with Dr. Martin Luther King Jr. to fight southern segregation policies. He also led the Southern Christian Leadership Conference (SCLC), an organization formed to bring an end to Black disenfranchisement and to advance the cause of civil rights in a nonviolent manner.

Young was born in New Orleans, Louisiana. He graduated from Howard University in Washington, D.C., and then attended Hartford Theological Seminary in Connecticut. Young was ordained as a minister in 1955 and moved to Georgia and became a pastor of the Evergreen Congregational Church in Beachton (near Thomasville).

In 1961, he moved to Atlanta and joined the SCLC to help organize voter registration drives in the South, where he became friends with King. On May 3, 1963, Young helped organize the anti-segregation march in Birmingham, Alabama, where Black children and other demonstrators were set upon by large dogs and fire hoses by order of Chief of Police Eugene "Bull" Connor. In response to the national newspaper and television coverage, protests came in from leaders all over the country. The events and subsequent public outcry motivated President John F. Kennedy to propose civil rights legislation that became the Civil Rights Act of 1964.

In 1964, Young became the SCLC's executive director. He worked alongside leaders in Washington, D.C., to draw up the Civil Rights Act of 1964 and the Voting Rights Act of 1965. Young was with Martin Luther King Jr. when the civil rights leader was assassinated in Memphis.

Andrew Young was elected to the House of Representatives in 1972, becoming the first African American chosen to represent Georgia since Reconstruction. He served three terms in Congress, during which time he led efforts to establish human rights programs and educational initiatives for the poor. In 1977, President Jimmy Carter chose Young to become the U.S. ambassador to the United Nations, where he advocated for human rights on the world stage.

Andrew Young. *Library of Congress.*

When he resigned the ambassadorship, he moved back to Georgia and ran for mayor of Atlanta, serving two terms from 1981 to 1988. Young and Billy Payne led the successful effort to host the Olympic Games in Atlanta in 1996. He wrote several books, including *An Easy Burden: The Civil Rights Movement and the Transformation of America.* He wrote and produced many documentaries and won the Peabody Institutional Award for Radio-Television Education for the programs *Look Up and Live*, *Pilgrimage*, *Frontiers of Faith* and *Talk-back.*

Throughout his life, Young earned many awards. Atlanta-based Morehouse College established the Andrew Young Center for Global Leadership in his honor. Nationally, he received the Presidential Medal of Freedom, and many colleges and universities have recognized him for his leadership in the cause for civil rights. He formed GoodWorks International supporting and consulting on development initiatives in Africa and other countries worldwide.

He famously said, "Freedom is a struggle, and we do it together. Not only together as Black citizens, but Black and white together."

Sources

Britannica. "Andrew Young, American Politician." www.britannica.com.

Fulton County Library System. Andrew Young papers. www.fulcolibrary.org/auburn-avenue-research-library.

Young, Andrew J., and Katir Sehgal. *Walk in My Shoes*. New York: MacMillan Press, 2010.

Young, Andrew, Harvey Newman and Andrea Young. *Andrew Young and the Making of Modern Atlanta*. Macon, GA: Mercer University Press, 2016.

ABOUT THE AUTHOR

Neely Young is a native of Cedartown, Georgia, a graduate of the University of Georgia and a proud journalist.

In 1968, he joined his family-owned newspaper, the *Valdosta Daily Times*, working in the photography department. After leaving Valdosta, he worked in various positions, and as both editor and publisher, for Georgia newspapers in Marietta, Canton, Dalton and Clayton County. In 1986, he became CEO of Morris Newspaper Corporation, which owned and operated forty newspapers in six states.

Three years later, Young formed Southern Publishing Co. with Tom Cousins, building a chain of thirteen newspapers over the course of nine years. In 1998, Southern Publishing was sold to Community Newspaper Holdings, but Young and Cousins were far from finished. The following year, in January 1999, they purchased *Georgia Trend* magazine, a publication with a circulation of fifty thousand that has become the state's go-to source for business, political and economic development information. Young served as the magazine's publisher and editor in chief for eighteen years until his retirement in 2017.

Young served as a curator for the Georgia Historical Society and often wrote about historical figures in his columns for *Georgia Trend* magazine. This book is a continuation of his long-standing interest in Georgia history and historical figures.

CPSIA information can be obtained
at www.ICGtesting.com
Printed in the USA
BVHW091227261021
619918BV00002B/123